Religious History

of

Ladakh

Bibliotheca Indo-Buddhica Series No. 215

Religious History
of
Ladakh

Prem Singh Jina (ed.)

Sri Satguru Publications
A Division of
Indian Books Centre
Delhi, India

Published by
Sri Satguru Publications,
Indological and Oriental Publishers
A Division of
Indian Books Centre
40/5, Shakti Nagar,
Delhi-110007
India

First Edition : Delhi, 2001

ISBN 81-7030-705-8

Published by Sunil Gupta for Sri Satguru Publications, a division of Indian Books Centre, 40/5, Shakti Nagar, Delhi-110007, India and printed at Chawla Offset Printers, Delhi 110 052

Dedicated to

MRS. MANJU JINA
MANVENDER JINA

CONTENTS

PREFACE

Ladakh has its unique importance as it is surrounded by some important republics of Central Asia viz. China, Afghanistan, Pakistan and Soviet Union. Because of delicate binding of Buddhist culture currents, Ladakh life style being infenence through the ages. Buddhist Missionaries for illustration came in Ladakh hundreds year before Christ. However. During 10th Century A.D. when Rin-chen-bzang-po visited Ladakh, Buddhism strongly hold its position, latter Ladakh Kings also patronaged this religion. Today Ladakh Autonomous Hill Development Council Leh has two main responsibilities – to preserve the Buddhist identity and to sustain the economic development.

The present volume is the product of three chapters written by the eminent scholars of Ladakh. The first Chapter deals with "The history of Christianity in Ladakh". In this chapter Fr. George Mampillil made a thorough study of Christianity in Ladakh since the arrival of St. Thomas the Apostte in 52 A.D. till today.

The second Chapter is written by Dr. Prem Singh Jina on "Buddhism in Ladakh". It offers an insight view of Buddhism in Ladakh. The author has referred several historical documents to substantiate his views.

Dr. Prem Singh Jina and Zain-ul-Abidin written third Chapter on "Islam in Ladakh". Authors in this paper endeavoured to search the process of Islamic cultural interaction in Buddhist society of Ladakh from ancient times to present days.

Therefore, this book covers the history of three religions viz. Buddhism, Christianity and Islam of Ladakh which will help the readers and researchers to know how Ladakh being influenced by the above religions in past and how the eco-cultural and religious changes are taking place in the passage of time? Thus this book will pave the way to study further the various aspects of religious cultural heritage of Ladakh.

Dr. Prem Singh Jina

ACKNOWLEDGEMENT

I owe a deep sense of gratitude to Prof. Maya Ram, Director Higher Education (Rtd.), Allahabad, U.P. for the encouragement given by him. I must thank Pt. Gautam Kaul, A.J.; Director General, Indo Tibetan Border Police, New Delhi for moral support. I am grateful to Prof. D.D. Sharma, Jawaharlal Nehru Fellow, T. Tashi (Tharik) of Chushod Shamma, Sonu Deol, P. Wangchok, Principal, Ladakh Public School, Leh; B.L. Raina, Sonam Wangchok, Lecturer in Hindi and Ishey Stanzin of Central Institute of Buddhist Studies, Leh-Ladakh for rendering help as and when required.

I am obliged to Dr. (Mrs.) Kapila vatsayayan (Academic Director) and M.C. Joshi, (Member Seceretary) Indira Gandhi National Centre for Arts, New Delhi, and Tondup Yangphel, Sr. Librarian, District Public Library, Leh, whose keen interest on Ladakh have always been a source of inspiration.

I would fail in performing my moral duties if I forget to mention Mrs. Manju Jina, Principal, Hira Convent School, Haldwani, who helped me in various ways in completing this book.

I am grateful to Fr. George Mampillil and Zain-ul-Abidin for contributing their learned papers for the present volume.

I am also grateful to the authors by whose thought and works, I have benefited immensely.

Dr. Prem Singh Jina

Chapter-I
THE HISTORY OF CHRISTIANITY IN LADAKH

Fr. George Mampillil

INTRODUCTION

Ladakh, the land of Lamas, mountain passes and freezing high desert in the trans Himalayan ranges of Kashmi: one of the remotest regions of India in the North. Virtually a land of arid valleys and snow clad mountains with peaks that rise above 20,000 feet, Ladakh is among the highest of the inhabited places in the world. Though remote never isolated, this barren land lying across the numerous cultural and religious influences from the mainland India, Tibet, Central Asia and even Europe. Invariably, Christianity also had its unique role to play India ever since the arrival of St. Thomas the Apostte in 52 A.D and was able to transform the lives of the people in various realms, Ladakh remained a land less trade by the Christian Missionaries till the latter half of the nineteenth century. Ever since its arrival in Ladakh the influence and the contribution of Christianity to the educational social and religious development of the people of the region have been of considerable importance. In the, following pages a study on Christianity in Ladakh in its historical perspective, is undertaken highlighting the milestones and the turning points in its past.

1. THE EARLIEST CHRISTIAN PRESENCE IN LADAKH

The earliest presence of Christian Missionaries in Ladakh can be traced back to 800 A.D. According to Rev. Yoseb Gergan, the author of *Ladags Rgyalrabs Chimed Ster* (History of Ladakh):

"In the year of our Lord Jesus 800, after his death Nestorian Christians of Syria have arrived this place from Samarkand (leader Charansar). In one year changed 215 camps to arrive Tangtse in Ladakh district about 60 miles east of Leh, after crossing 18,000 ft. high from Leh"[1].

Here Gergan's versatility need not be doubted cause Samarkand was a flourishing Centre of Nestorian Christians[2]. Dominic Thirunilath further strengthened Yoseb Gergan's statement about Nestorian Christians appearance in Ladakh during 8th century A.D., as he writes :

"From the fourth to seventh Century Nestorian and Armanian Mission, penetrated Mongolia, Chinese Turkistan and probably Tibet. The writing of the early Tibetan Missionaries are full of reference to the existence of Christianity in the mystical land of Tibet even prior to the introduction of Buddhism. The religious organization, creed and rituals are there to confirm that St. Thomas the Apostte crossal into that country to preach the Gospel and that the Christian faith was the religion of the people----- The early merchants and travellers in their wandering across the plains and uplands of Central Asia witnessed the presence of Christian symbols and ceremonies".[3]

The Christian presence in Ladakh during 8th Century A.D. can further be proved by three carved crosses in the persian style with Syriac inscriptions on a rock in Tangtse. Mar Aprrem writes:

"Three crosses are seen in Tibet (Western Tibet, or better Known as Ladakh). On the top of the cross there is a Syrian inscription which reads ISHOW. The three crosses on the left hand side of a big rock are of the Persian style usually known as the Nestorian cross. On the right hand side of these three crosses, there are Syriac inscriptions written in vertical lines".[4]

However, it wouldn't have been an impossible missions for the Missionaries of the Nestorian Church, often described as "a Church on fire" to be prompted by the great commission of Jesus, (Mt. 28: 19-20) to undertake an adventurous Mission to the roof of the world as early as 800 A.D.

Dr. Sebastian Vadakel who visited Tangtse in 1996, writes :

"As we went up the Himalayan mountain ranges crossing many passes the thought that predominated my mind was the courage and zeal of the early Missionaries of the "Church on fire" who on foot went along that path preaching the Gospel and leaving behind them the perenial testimonies of their vibrant Christian faith".[5]

"On one rock there are three crosses engaged side by side. On the top of another rock there are many crosses of different shape and size. Vertical writing in Syriac script is seen in two places. The script is illegible except for the word 'Ishow' written under one of the crosses".[6]

Unfortunately we do not know much about this 8th Century Missionary endeavours of the Nestorian Christian in Tangtse. The carved crosses with Syriac inscription remain as the perenial testimonies of the presence of Christianity as early as 800 A.D. unless measures are taken to conserve even these legacies of the past Christian presence could be destroyed and lost in the course of time.

2. THE MORVIAN CHURCH IN LADAKH

The Missionaries of the Moravian Church[7] had an ambitious plan of starting mission work in the Himalayan Kingdom of Mongolia.[8] This great Missionary endeavour was popularly referred to as the Himalaya Mission. In 1853 two pioneers of the Himalayan Mission. Edward Pagell and Welhelm Heyde, set out to Mongolia and reached Ladakh on their way. They hoped to reach their destination by crossing Tibet and made three attempts to cross the Tibetan territory but to no avail. They were not allowed by the Maharaja of Kashmir to settle down in Ladakh either.[9] These events ultimately led to the founding of a mission station at Kyelong in the year, 1856[10]. They kept a regular contact with Ladakh till they could start one Mission station there in 1885.[11]

2.1 The Moravian Christians at Kyelong (HP)

Kyelong in the Lahul Spiti region of the present Himachal Pradesh was visited by many Ladakhi traders. There were also many Ladakhis who sought refuge in Kyelong to escape from the high taxes levied by the Maharaja of Kashmir. All those who became Christians as late as 1889 were from to embrace the Christian faith were Sonam Stobgyes and his son Samuel Jolden in 1865.[12]

Meanwhile the missionary activities of Pagell and Heyde were enhanced by the addition of Heinrich August Jaeschke, a talented linguist, to the mission staff. In 1858 Heyde obtained a printing press from Shimla. The other activities of the Mission were the farm under the supervision of Heyde; the school opened in 1861 and the knitting training centre. The large model farm, in the course of time, was rented out to the indigenous Christians who began to consider it as a reward for embracing Christianity creating a confusion between the spiritual and material aims of Christianity. In addition the local land lords opposed the activities of the Missionaries even to the extend of organizing a boycott against the Christians in 1938. In the words of John Bray:

"In 1940 a combination of internal weakness and external pressure led to its (Kyelong Mission Station's) closure."

Thus the ambitious Missionary endeavour of the great Moravian pioneers, Edward Pagell and Welhelm Heyde became non-existent in Kyelong as the three indigenous Christian families moved to Leh and the remaining handful returned to their old faith.[14]

2.2 The Poo Mission Station

Edward Pagell and Welhelm Heyde, extending their work, founded another Mission in 1865 at Poo on the upper Sutlej near the Tibetan border.[15] Poo with the strength of 64 local Christians by the year 1908 proved to be a promising station. Though in policy the Missionaries would not want to convert any seeking material benefits they had to assist the local Christians by securing employment and providing food grains as all of them were of poor financial status. In such a situation catering to the spiritual as well as other needs of the faithful became a laborious task and the possibility of the further expansion of the Missionary activities seemed practically impossible. In such a situation assisting a Mission station for and dependent like Poo proved to be impractical. As John Bray says:

"The Mission station was closed down in 1924 and almost all the indigenous Christians lapsed back into Buddhism".[16]

2.3 The Moravian Mission at Leh :

As the Kyelong Christian community comprised of the people originally from Ladakh who took refuge in Kyelong, they had an ardent desire to return to their homeland. At least two Christian families had come back to Ladakh in 1882. Opening a Mission station at Leh became a pressing need for the Missionaries to cater to the pastoral needs of the faithful who were returning to Ladakh. Moreover, Ladakh was a flourishing trade centre. Having been personally supported by the British Viceroy the request of the Moravian Missionaries was granted by the Maharaja of Kashmir in 1884 which paved the way for opening a Mission at Leh in the year, 1885[17]. The first resident Missionary, F. Redslob, arrived at Leh in 1885. In the very next year the first Moravian Church was built which is in existence upto this day. In the following year (i.e. 1887) F. Redslob started the Moravian Mission School at Leh.[18] Dr. Karl Marx took up the responsibility of the hospital and clinic. This stupendous growth of the Mission at Leh came to a screeching halt when both Dr. Karl Marx and F. Redslob died of thypus within a few days of each other in 1891. The timely intervention of Becker shawe and Julias Weber brought about the survival of the Leh Mission. Two other Missionaries to join them were S.H. Ribbach in 1894 and A.H. Francke, the historian cum scholar, in 1896. The recovery of the Mission from the severe blow in 1891 was slow but steady and by way of expending the Missionary endeavour a substation was opened in Khalatse (or Kha-la-che) by A.H. Francke assisted by the evangelist Chompel, in the year 1899. Though the starting of the world war-I hampered the activities of the German Missionaries at Leh and Kyelong the presence of the British and Swiss Missionaries was of great help to the Mission.[19]

The year 1920 was a turning point in the history of the Moravian Church in Ladakh. In October of the same year Bishop Arthur ward of the London Mission Board declared that the Moravian Church in Ladakh would become self dependent and ordained Rev. Yoseb Gergan and Rev. Dewazung Dana as the first two Ladakhi Ministers. The main emphasis from then onwards was in the words of John Bray:

"Hastening the self-dependence of the indigenous Church as well as gathering new converts."[20]

Bishop Arthur ward exhorted in 1920 that :

"The Leh Church should be responsible for its own affairs within a generation."[21]

In fact Leh being the headquarter of Ladakh the Christians there had many favourable circumstances unlike those at Kyelong. Poo, and Khaltse (Kha-la-che). Within its cosmopolitan environment the followers of other faith such as the Buddhists, Muslims and Hindus lived with their Christian brethren in religious harmony and peace. Availing themselves of the comparatively better educational facilities and employment opportunities the christians could produce able leaders in the society and thus distinguished themselves as a "Unitas Fratrum" to reckon with.

2.4. The Moravian Christians at Shey (Sheh) and Khalatse (Kha-la-che)

Started as an out station Sheh was under the pastoral cure of the Minister at Leh till 1937. It became a full fledged Mission station in 1940 with a resident evangelist. The Moravian community at Sheh held their Sunday services in the annexe built by Shamul over his stable. In 1962 a Church was built at Sheh. The present new Church cum the parsonage was built in 1998 and was blessed on 20th, September of the same year by Rev. W.J.H. McOwat, the Chairman of the British Mission Board. At present there are seven christian families at Sheh. Rev. Dechen Chamgha has been catering to the spiritual needs of the people since 1990.

The Moravian Christian community at Khalatse (Kha-la-che), though started in 1899, has now only a handful of the faithful from three families. The resident Pastor Rev. Samson Thangpa has been in charge of the Khalatse (Kha-la-che) congregation since 1998.

2.5 Some concerns of the Mission

There were some serious social and pastoral concerns that the Christians had to face in Ladakh. One of the most important concerns was the loss of the faithful through marriage between Christian and non-Christian spouses and emigration. Parochial disputes and internal quarrels also disturbed the unity of the Christian community. Still another factor of concern was the question of declining authority and power of the Missionaries over the faithful. Moreover, the low regard of the Missionaries for the Ladakhis' administrative skill and their fear that the indigenous Christian leaders might fail to sustain the high standard of religious discipline made them reluctant to devolve the powers to the local Church administrators. As a result there was an increasing Ladakhi resentment of the authoritarian foreign leaders combined with a sense of dependency on them.[22] In 1940's with considerable difficulties Walter Asboe and Norman Driver persuaded the Leh congregation to become financially independent.

After the independence of India, the partition of the country and the subsequent riot the socio-political situation in Ladakh returned to normalcy by 1949. As the stay of the foreign Missionaries at Leh, after the independence, was uncertain the Ladakhi Christians were prepared in full swing to take over the full responsibility of the Church. The last European Missionaries Pierre and Catherine Vittoz stayed at Leh from 1950 to 1956. In the year 1951 E.T. Phunthsog[23] had joined the Mission staff while Yonathan Paljor was undergoing training in the Theological College, Saharanpur, U.P. In 1956 Bishop Cannor visited Ladakh and Ordained both E.T. Phunthsog and Yonathan Paljor as the Ministers for the Leh Church. But in spite of its Indian leadership the Moravian Church of Ladakh to a certain extent, depended on her European counterpart Pursuing the noble but short-lived attempts made by Elijah Phunthsog back in 1950s, the Church in Ladakh is yet to find ways and means to explain the Christian faith in terms intelligible to the Ladakhi mind which is basically Buddhist in its religious and social out look.

2.6. The Contribution of the Moravian Church

Though a micro-minority in the trans-Himalayan region of Kashmir and living amidst the diverse socio-cultural scenario and age old indigenous religion-philosophical milieu of Buddhism, the Moravian Church's contribution in the field of literature, health care and education are commendable and praise worthy.

2.6. (a) Literature

One of the renowned personalities who contributed greatly to the field of literature is Heinrich August Jaeschke who came to Ladakh in 1857 and started his pioneering the research into Tibetan language and literature.[25] He translated most of the New Testament books into Tibetan and brought out a series of linguistic works. He published the first English Tibetan dictionary in 1881.[26] Jaeschke was succeeded by F.A. Redslob who took to the translation of the Old Testament books in 1880s. He was assisted by Nathaniel Zodpa Gyaltsen and Gergan Sonam. After the departure of F.A. Redslob a committee of European and Ladakhi translators at Leh continued his noble task in the early 1900s.[27] Welhelm Heyde, the pioneering Missionary in Ladakh had already begun in 1898 his revision of the Tibetan New Testament with a group of Tibetan scholars in Darjeeling. Meanwhile A.H. Francke brought out the translation of St. Mark's Gospel in Ladakhi and in Lahoul (Lahuli) dialects of Bunam and Manchad. Rev. Yoseb Gergan took up the task of translating the remaining books of the old Testamenent, something which became his life long Mission. The landmark in the evolution of the Tibetan-Christian literature was, indeed, the publication of the Tibetan Bible in 1948. In 1950 E.T. Phunthsog and P. Pierre Vittoz published a revised version of the New Testment.[28]

Apart from the strictly Christian literature in Tibetan language there were other valuable contributions by the Moravian Missionaries in the field of literature. It was Dr. Karl Marx who made a serious attempt to study the Ladakhi history and published three Ladakhi Chronicles. He was followed by A.H. Francke who wrote more than 60 scholarly articles on various topics as Ladakhi languages, legends, songs, rock carvings and archeology. The first Ladakhi news papers "The Ladakhi News" was started by him in 1904. The literary contributions of Rev. Yoseb Gergan include an acrostic poem, two booklets entitled: 'The Spectacle of Human Souls' (1925) and 'Understandable Expressions of Moral Thoughts' (1925); a pumphlet, 'An abridged ceremonies and a collection of Tibetan proverbs.[29] His historical researches were edited and published posthumously as 'Ladags Rgyalrabs Chimed Ster' by his son S.S. Gergan in 1976.[30]

Another personality who made remarkable contributions in the field of literature was Walter Asboe who had a hobby of writing in his spare time. Apart from a series of narratives on life in Ladakh in the Moravian Mission magazine he published learned papers in Scholarly journals. In 1936 he came over to Leh and edited the Ladakhi News which was again revived by E.T.Phunthsog in 1950. E.T. Phunthsog's attempts to promote a new way of writing Ladakhi phonetically, instead of using the Tibetan alphabets, was not welcomed by the Government authorities and the people in general.[31]

2.6 (b) Health Care

The Moravian Missionaries considered health care to be a valuable area of service to the masses and as a means to get in touch with the people around them. Dr. Karl Marx was a fully trained doctor who arrived at Leh in April 1887 to take over the responsibilities of the Mission hospital and clinic. In the summer medical tours were arranged to far flung areas to conduct cataract operation and to provide medical aid to the villagers. The 'Zenana Mission' was yet another feature of the Missionaries health care work. It was a reach-out programme organized by the wives of the Missionaries and the unmarried women workers to reach medical assistance to the Muslim women folk of Leh. This medical work had a social and religious dimensions as well.[32]

In 1920 there were two qualified doctors Dr. S.R. Heber and his wife in the Mission hospital But Dr. Heber resigned his post in 1925 as, John Bray says :

"He had too little to do because the Ladakhis were too healthy."[33]

After the departure of Dr. Heber and his wife, Dr. Berry extended his service to the Mission hospital until the arrival of Dr. Mary Shawe in 1930. She served the Mission for the next twenty two years and moved over to Khalatse (Kha-la-che) in 1952 after her marriage with Norman Driver and would visit Leh to hold Clinics from time to time. In the course of time the existence of the government hospital made the Mission less important as a medical centre.[34]

2.6 (c) Education :

The Moravian Missionaries played an important role in the area of education in Ladakh as the schools did have significant roles to play in all Moravian Missions elsewhere. As there was no Govt. School at Leh till 1889 an edit was issued by Radha Kishan, the then Governor of Kashmir that every family with more than one child should send one to the Mission school. The total number of students in the Mission schools at Leh, Kyelong and Poo had risen to 275 by 1901. The Children were sent to school only in the winter as they were kept busy shepherding and doing other household works in the summer. Moreover, the benefits of education was not properly understood by the masses[35]. The opening of the first Govt. school at Leh in 1911 lowered the number of students in the Mission school as the classes in the Govt. school went to higher standards and the medium of instruction was Urdu the state language of Jammu & Kashmir. The education of girls in 1920s was an area where the Missionaries made great contributions. Practical education for women was given through the training centres for knitting organized by the wives of the Missionaries.[36]

A new initiative in the filed of education was taken by Walter Asboe in 1939 when he started the Leh Industrial school for training the people in handicrafts especially in the art of Tibetan carpet weaving. Though short-lived (1937-47) this endeavour produced skilled craftmen for the Govt. Handicraft Centers.[37]

Starting of the Govt. run educational institutions caused a decline in the educational activities of the Mission. The school continued until 1960 with a handful of students, and later, on account of various internal and external reasons, the educational activities of the Moravian Mission came to a standstill in Ladakh. After a twenty year long gap the Moravian Mission school at Leh was reopened for students upto class three, under the able leadership of Nathaniel Batapa in the early 1980s. The school was upgraded with the Govt. recognition for courses upto class 10 under Stephen Ishey. In May 1996 a rural branch of the school with classes upto standard five was opened at Matho village. Today with an overall student body of about 1300. Moravian Mission School stands under the able leadership of Rev. Elijah Spalbar Gergan as one of the best educational institutions in the Ladakh region.[38]

2.6. (d) Evangelization :

The primary aim of the Moravian Missionaries when they decided to settle down at Kyelong (1855) and later at Leh (1885) was evangelization.[39] In other words they came to preach the Gospel, the good news of salvation brought about by the Saviour Jesus Christ. They got involved in active preaching ministry. A good number of non-christians also would gather to listen to the preaching in the Mission Church. There were special gatherings on every Friday evening mainly for the non-Christians when the Bible stories were narrated with the help of slide shows. In the summer the Missionaries made preaching tours, distributing tracts and extracts from the Bible to the remote areas. They undertook such preaching tours in the words John Bray:

"For scatterinmg the seed of the Gospel over a wide area in the hope that even a few seeds might germinate".[40]

Thus in the course of the time this task was entrusted with the local evangelists based in remote valleys away from the Mission station. Bishop F.E. Peter reported in 1928 that each member of his preaching team of indigenous evangelists spent 90 days on the road in the year 1927. Travelling in disguise as traders some of them reached upto Rudok in Tibet and to Chinese Turkestan. Apart from the magic lantern they used scrolls painted in Buddhist Thangka style as preaching aids. Following the Buddhist tradition they sometimes carved Bible passages on the wayside rocks.[41]

The minstrel trips were new missionary endeavours initiated by Pierre Vittoz and E.T. Phuntsog in early 1950s. They encouraged the use of pictures and Christian songs composed in Ladakhi tunes. This ministries tried to bear witness to the fact that "Christianity doesn't mean wealth and European habits but joyful service".[42] The seeds of the Gospel scattered by the Missionaries brought about good harvest. Though the Moravian Christian community still remains small in number. There were as per the Moravian Almanac, 1984, 140 communicants and a total membership of 400. Since 1990, Rev. Elijah Spalbar Gergan looks after the spiritual needs of the faithful of the Leh Congregation.

3. THE CATHOLIC MISSIONARY ENDEAVOURS IN LADAKH

Here follow details of Catholic Missionary activities.

3.1 The Society of Jesus (During 17th-18th Centuries):

During 17th Century till 18th Century a few Catholic Missionaries passed through Ladakh, here follow the details:

3.1 (a) Antonio de Andrade :

The first Catholic Missionary to pass through Ladakh in the early 1620s was the Jesuit priest Antonio de Andrade who was infact on a laborious expedition in search of the lost Christian community in Tibet. From the early middle ages onwards there were rumours of lost communities of Christians in Central Asia vaguely associated with the name of the mythical emperor Prester John.[43] Such reports were also based on a superficial and outward similarity of some Buddhist ceremonies to those of the Catholic Church.[44] Andrade was successful in establishing a Catholic Mission in Tsaparang with the whole hearted support of the King of Guge.[45] However the Mission was short-lived due to a revolt against the King of Guge by displeased lamas with the support of the Ladakhi King.[46] The Guge King was defeated and the Ladakhis took him into an honourable exile to Leh in 1630. Two of the Missionaries were also taken prisoners to Leh but later released and allowed to return to Tsaparang.[47] Antonio de Andrade left no mark of his visit to Leh.

3.1 (b) Francesco de Azevedo and Giovanni de Oliverio :

In 1631 two Jesuit Missionaries : Francesco de Azevedo and Giovanni de Oliverio visited Ladakh. As they did not have a Mission in Ladakh their stay there was short.[48] In fact, Azevedo was appointed by Antonio de Andrade, the then head of the Jesuit Mission province of Goa, as a visitor to the Tsaparang Mission after receiving the first report (1631) of the revolution there. Azevedo found that the only means of reestablishing the Tsaparang Mission was to gain the favour of the Ladakhi King Singhe Namgyal (seṅ ge rnam-rgyal) and therefore he undertook a journey to Leh. Regarding the journey of Azevedo, C. Wessels writes :

"It was impossible (for Azevedo) to do anything here (Tsaparang) for the new governor was very hostile to the Mission. So Azevedo made up his mind to go to Leh and treat personally with the King---- he chose Oliverio as his companion and interpretor and on October 4, in 1631, the caravan took the road to Leh and reached Leh after twenty one days travelling from sunrise to sunset."[49]

Therefore even if the Tsaparang Mission could not recover from the severe blow of 1630 the Ladakhi King Singhe Namgyal (Seṅge-rnam-rgyal) treated the Missionaries with respect and sent them away with the promise that they could carry on their work in Guge, Rudok and even at Leh. After staying at Leh a short span of fifteen days the two Missionaries left Leh on 7th November, 1631 for Agra via Thung-Lung (Taglangla), Bara-Lacha and Rohtang passes at times floundering through breast-deep high snow.[50]

3.1 (c) Hippolytus Desideri :

The next Catholic Missionary to reach Ladakh was Hippolytus Desideri, and Italian Jesuit. He was appointed by the head of Jesuit Mission in Goa for the noble task of reopening the Tibetan Mission assisted by another Jesuit priest Manuel Freyre from Delhi. Regarding this Desideri himself writes:

"Having been appointed to the Tibetan Mission I left Goa on 20th of November, 1713 and arrived at Surat on 4th of January 1714. On the 26th of March I set out for Delhi where I arrived on the 11th of May and I joined company with Father Manuel Freyre who had been appointed to the same Mission as myself."[51]

Therefore having spent the winter in Srinagar they set out eastward to Ladakh in the month of May 1715 Desideri writes :

"We had left Kashmir on the 17th of May.... The journey from Kashmir to Ladakh we made on foot and it lasted forty days so that we reached the last named place on the 25th of June."[52]

On their arrival at Leh Desideri was confused as Ladakh was very much alike Tibet and therefore he called Ladakh as the "Second Tibet". Misunderstanding the proper name of Leh, the capital of Ladakh, he called it "Lhata". He writes:

"We arrived at the city of Leh, also with the other name of Lhata, which is the capital of the Second Tibet."[53]

However, both the lamas of the faith of Jesus Christ were given a hearty welcome by the Ladakhi King Nyima Namgyal (Ni-ma-rnam rgyal), so much so that Desideri was willing to settle down in the Kingdom of the hospitable King in order to start a Mission there. He also found that the people were well disposed to the Christian faith. Desideri writes:

"The King and many of his court look upon us as lamas of the faith of Jesus Christ.... this people is well disposed to taste of the Christian truths. On the second of July we had our first audience of the King himself who received us seated on his throne. On the 4th and 8th we were again summoned to his presence and he then treated us more familiarly. On the 6th paid our respects to the Grand lama. He was accompanied by several other lamas.... They received us most honourably and presented us with some refreshments as is the custom of the country."[54]

However, Desideri's superior, Manuel Freyre, more accomsted to the life in the plains of India and worn out attar the tedious journey to Leh, was only most willing to abandon the enterprise of founding a Mission at Leh. As he found that there was no possibility of returning to the plains by another route, after two months stay at Leh, it was resolved to push on to Lhasa.[55]

Thus the Catholic Missionary endeavour to Ladakh in the early seventeenth and eighteenth centuries came to a standstill.

3.2. The Second Phase of the Catholic Missionary Endeavour in Ladakh.

3.2 (a) The Mill Hill Mission (1888-1898):

Bifurcating the diocese of Lahore (Pakistan) the Prefecture Apostolic of Kashmir and Kafirstan was erected in the year 1887 and the same was entrusted to the Mill Hill Mission.[56] Ladakh was one of their very first Mission areas. In the year 1888 Fr. Daniel Kilty reached Ladakh with the necessary permission from the British Resident in Kashmir, to stay in Ladakh until August 1890, in order to learn language. Initially staying is the Dak Bungalow he started an intensive language study. Meanwhile a house was constructed from him at the Govt. expense. He lived a life of austerity which effected to a collapse of his health. The three roomed house was used as his living room. Chapel and a Class room for the few local boys he gathered to educate. It was named St. Peter's Mission. Moreover, his intensive language study culminated into making a new dictionary. However, he took to ill by the Spring of 1889 and at the age of

34, on 23 April, the Tuesday after Easter he died of exhaustion due to liver abcess.[57]

A group of four Mill Hill Missionaries– Frs. Ignatius Brouwer, Joseph Cunnigham, Henry Hanlon and Michal Donsan– reached Leh on 8th Sept. 1890, because the Mission superior Fr. Ignatius Brouwer judged that, "Kilty's initiatives at Leh to be too important not to be pursued further."[58] Among the four fathers Hanlong and Donsen stayed at Leh from 1890-95 continuing Fr. Kilty's Mission. They embarked and serious study of the Ladakhi language, customs and religious beliefs. As they acquired a workable knowledge of the language they engaged in humanitarian as well as evangelization works.[59]

3.2 (b) Missionaries : Catholic and Moravian :

Catholic and Moravian Missionary activities in past were similar in many respects. In their Missionary method both had combined evangelization with educational and medical work, and embarked upon preaching tours to far flung villages. There was similarity also in the response of the Ladakhis that both Missions received. Buddhists in Ladakh argued that :

"Each one to the religion of his birth and your religion is good enough for you but Buddhism is the best religion."[60]

Thus both the Missions faced the same problems of pressure from the Buddhist monasteries and social obstacles against conversion.

Regarding the relationship between the two Missions it could be rightly said that it was one of competition rather than co-operation.[61] Hanlon made it a point to ensure that the people understood the difference between the Catholic and Moravian Churches. The Moravian Missionary method of distributing the Tibetan translation of the Gospel was not that acceptable to the Catholic Missionaries, because the Ladakhis were likely to misinterpret the Scripture unless they had proper guidance.[62] This sort of mutual tension between the Catholic and Moravian Missionaries was typical of their time.

3.2 (c), The Closure of the Second Phase of the Catholic Mission in Ladakh

Henry Hanlon was called back to Rawalpindi in 1893 and was ordained and appointed as the first Roman Catholic Bishop of Uganda in the year, 1894. Ignatius Brouwer not willing to leave Michal Donsen alone at Leh, withdrew him to Baramulla (Kashmir) in 1894. He returned to Ladakh in the summer of 1894 and 1895. He was called back to Rawalpindi and later he returned to Europe in 1899 because of health reasons. Meanwhile Fr. D.J. Reyders had been appointed as the Mission superior in the place of

Ignatius Brouwer. Considering the reasons like shortage of man power, unfavourable social and religious circumstances and the apparent fruitlessness of the ten years of labours spent in Ladakh the Prefecture Apostolic of Kashmir and Kafirstan made a formal decision to close the Catholic Mission in Ladakh.[63]

3.3. The Third Phase of the Catholic Missionary Endeavour in Ladakh: The Missionary Society of St. Thomas the Aposthe – 1995.

Reopening of the Ladakh Mission was a dream so dear to Bishop Hippolytus Kunnunleal ofm. Cap. the first Bishop of Jammu-Srinagar Diocese.[64] A team headed by Dr. Peter Calestine visited Ladakh on 7th Sept. 1978 to explore the possibilities of reopening the Ladakh Mission. In July, 1981 another team of Missionaries under the leadership of Msgr.Hippolytus Kunnunkal and the Archoishop Angelo Fernandes of Delhi visited Ladakh. They met many important people of Ladakh and offered Holy Mass in several Military Churches. They also participated in the liturgical service of the Moravian Church, Leh and placed a provisional slab to commemorate the memory of Fr. Daniel Kilty M.H.M., who was buried at Leh in 1889. After a couple of months Fr. Dominic T., the Parish priest of the Holy Family Church, Srinagar visited Leh and made negotiations with the Govt. Officials to open a Mission station at Leh.[65] Meanwhile Bishop Hippolytus Kunnunkal had requested Mother Terasa to send Sisters to work in Ladakh. Mother Terasa sent two M.C. Sisters to visit Leh along with Frs. Joseph K. and Jose John on 24 August, 1992.[66]

In his search of the personnel to reopen the Catholic Mission in Ladakh Bishop Hippolytus wrote to Rev. Dr. Sebastian Vadakel, the Director General of the Missionary Society of St. Thomas the Apostle (M.S.T.) requesting him to take up the Challenge of the Ladakh Mission. The response of the MST was in affirmative and Rev. Dr. Sebastian Vadakel MST and Fr. John Kadookunnel MST along with Dr. Peter Celestine, Fr. P.M. George, Mr. Preduman K. Joseph Dhar, the former Principal of Govt. Higher Secondary School, Leh visited Ladakh in from 19 to 26th June, 1994 with the sole purpose of exploring the possibilities to re-establish the Catholic Mission in Ladakh.[67] The decision of the Diocesan Council to entrust the Ladakh region to the MST for an experimental period of two years, was conveyed to the Director General through a letter dated 17th November, 1994. Fr. Lanappan Arangassery, Fr. Stanly Ambukunnel and Fr. Sebastian Cherickanampurath Volunteered to go to Ladakh.

Again in November, 1994 Dr. Peter Celestine and Mr. Bhushanlal Das came to Leh to make immediate arrangements for the residence of the three

MST fathers. They made an agreement with Mrs. Elza Joldan and her two-storeyed building at the Fort Road, Leh was rented out for one year. They made another agreement with Mrs. Miriam Zangpo of Sheh Village to construct a house and hand it over to the MST fathers on lease for five year. Two other persons who extended valuable service towards the reopening of the Catholic Mission in Leh were Maj Victor Walter and his sister Ms. Helen Walter from Calcutta; Maj. Walter had quit army in 1991 and started various social service activities supported by Ms. Helen. In 1997 Maj. Victor Walter left for Rome to study for priesthood and Ms. Helen went back to Calcutta.[68]

The long cherished dream of Bishop Hippolytus Kunnunkal was realized on 3rd July, 1995 when St. Peter's Catholic Mission was reopened by the fathers of the Missionary Society of St. Thomas the Apostle. Fr. Lonappan Arangassery, Fr. Stanly Ambukunnel and Fr. Sebastian Cherickanampurath. The Taberancle of the Lord was placed and the santury lamp lit in the presence of Fr. Peter Celestine, the delegate of Bishop Hippolytus Kunnunkal, Fr. P.M. George the Diocesan procurator any other dignitories.[69]

Fr. Mathew Moothasseril MST reached Leh on 18th August, 1995 to take up the responsibility as the leader of the MST team at Leh and Fr. Lonappan Arangassery MST left for Kerala on 25th August, 1995. Apart from catering to the spiritual needs of the Military personnel, the MST fathers started English Coaching Class for the High School and College students. Meanwhile the residence of the fathers was shifted to Sheh. A piece of land was brought near Choglamsar and the School construction work started on 3rd Sept. 1997. In the year, 1998 the members of the pioneering team were transferred and replaced by another team of Fr. Joseph Mullappillil MST (April, 1998), Fr. George Mampillil MST (May, 1998) under the leadership of Fr. Jose Kalarickal MST (October, 1998).

CONCLUSION

The historical actuality of founding of Christian community in this trans-Himalayan region of Ladakh back in 1880s by the Moravian Missionaries and the bold attempts made as 800 A.D by the Nestorian Missionaries and then in early seventeenth, eighteenth and late nineteenth centuries by the Catholic Missionaries remain a fascinating subject of research and serious study for any student on the religious history of this "Little Tibet". Though not, exclusive an attempt has been made in the above pages to shed new light on the history of Christianity in Ladakh.

Even at the threshold of the third Christian millennium the Christian population of Ladakh is only a micro-minority. Though the Church has not spread and flourished as the pioneering Missionaries would have wished, the very fact that the pains taken by them to scatter the seeds of the Gospel have not been in vain, is a promising factor.

FOOT NOTES & REFERENCES

1. Gergan, Yoseb: 'Ladags Rgyalrabs Chimed Ster' (History of Ladakh), New Delhi, Sterling Pub. 1976.
2. Around 800 A.D. Samarkand was the seat of a Metropolitan. There were Bishops in Khotan and Yarkand. The Zealous Christians under their Bishop and Metropolitians had undertaken an ambitions Mission to Tangtse near Leh. Mar Apram 'Nestorian Missions', Trichur, Mar Narsai Press, 1976.
3. Thirunilath, Dominic, 'A Cursory Glance of the Early History of Christianity' In Christianity in Jammu & Kashmir, Vishinath Press, P. 10
4. Aprem, Mar: 'Nestorian Missions', P. 100
5. Vadakel, Sebastian: 'A Pilgrimage to Tangtse on the Chinese Boarder', Santhome Mission, Vol. III, No. 4, 1996, P. 13
6. Ibid, P. 15
7. The upheaval that caused the origin of the Moravian Church can be traced back to the early fifteenth Century in Germany in the year, 1457. John Hus, a member of the faculty of the University of Prague raised his voice against selling of Indulgences and other malpractices of the Church. He was declared a heretic and was burnt at stake in 1415. His followers Known as Hussites rose in revolt. But they were severely persecuted in following nearly 40 years. In the course of time the followers of John Hus found themselves unable to agree on many points and no single leader emerged who could keep the variant factions together. Finally a small group broke away and established a faternity known as Moravia, Germany. This Unitas Fratrum later came to be known as the Moravian Church.

   Cf. Bray, John: 'The Moravian Church in Ladakh : The First forty year, 1885-1925, Detlef Kantowsky (ed) IN: Recent Research on Ladakh: History, Culture, Sociology, Ecology, London: Weltforum Verlag Munchan-Koln, 1981, P. 282 & Graenfeldt, John 'The Moravian Church, P.2.
8. From the early decade of the 18th Century onwards the attention of the Moravian Missionaries had been turned towards the Kalmuk and Mongol tribes and in 1765 a Moravian settlement was formed near Czarizin on the Volga, This Missionary endeavour had to be terminated due to the interference of the Russian Government in 1821.

   Cf. Clements R. Markhan, Narratives of the Mission of George Bogle to Tibet and of the Journey of Thomas Manning to Lhasa, New Delhi : Manjusri Publishing House, 1971, P.C. viii
9. Ladakh was not a part of the British India but was under the dominion of the Hindu Maharaja of Kashmir.

Cf. Alastair Lamn, 'Kashmir: A Disputed Legacy 1846-1990, Karachi Oxford University Press, 1993 P. 26.

10. Clements R. Markaham, Narratives of the Mission of George Bogle to Tibet, P. CVII
11. Jina, Prem Singh: 'Famous Western Explorers to Ladakh' New Delhi, Indus Publishing Co. 1995 PP. 37, 38
12. Bray, John: 'The Moravian Church in Ladakh : 1885-1925, Op. Cit. P. 82
13. Bray, John: 'Christianity in Ladakh : The Moravian Church from 1920 to 1956' In : 'Ladakh Himalaya Accidental Ethologie, Ecologie' : Pau, France, 1985: PP 207-220.
14 Ibid.
15. Bray, John: 'The Moravian Church in Ladakh : 1885-1925', P, 82
16. Bray, John: "Christianity in Ladakh : The Moravian Church from 1920-56', P. 213
17. Bray, John: 'The Moravian Church Ladakh : 1985-1925', Op. Cit. P. 82.
18. Jina, Prem Singh: 'Famous Western Explorers to ladakh', Op. Cit. P. 64
19. Bray, John: 'The Moravian Church in Ladakh : 1885-1925', Op. Cit. P. 83
20. Bray, John: 'Christianity in Ladakh: 1920-56', P.2
21. Ibid, P. 214
22. Ibid, P. 215
23. Kundan, T.Z: 'A Christian from Ladakh Bobility: Elijah Thsetan Phuntsog', In: Christianity in Jammu & Kashmir', Kashmir, Vishinath, Press, PP. 80-81.
24. Bray, John: 'Christianity in Ladakh: 1920-56', PP. 215-216.
25. 'A Missionary to Western Tibetans: Henray Au-Augusts Jaeschko:', In: 'Christianity in Jammu and Kashmir', Op. Cit. P. 82.
26. Moravian Mission Vol. 27, No. 10, Oct. 1929, P. 80
27. Bray, John: 'Christianity in Ladakh : 1920-56', P. 210
28. Ibid & John Bray: 'The Moravian Church in Ladakh: 1895-1925'; Op, Cit. PP. 82-85
29. Bray John: 'Christianity in Ladakh : 1920-56', Op. Cit.P.211.
30. Gergan, Yoseb; Op. Cit., 1976
31. Bray, John : 'The Moravian Church in Ladakh: 1885-1925' and 'Christianity in Ladakh: 1920-56, Op. Cit. P. 211.
32. Bray, John: 'The Moravian Church in Ladakh: 1885-1925', Op. Cit. P. 86
33. Bray, John: 'Christianity in Ladakh: 1885-1925', Op.Cit. P. 208
34. Ibid.
35. Bray, John : 'The Moravian Church in Ladakh: 1885-1925, Op.Cit.P.87
36. Ibid, PP. 87-88

37. Bray, John : 'Christianity in Ladakh : 1920-56' Op. Cit. P. 209
38. School Diary of Moravian Mission School, Leh, 1998, PP-4-5
39. Etimologically the word evangelization in derived from the Greek term, 'Evangelion' of which the Latin translation is 'evangelium' which means Good News or Gospel.

    Cf. Jacob Kattackal, 'An Introduction to Bible' Aluva, St. Joseph, Press, 1980.
40. Bray, John : 'The Moravian Church in Ladakh: 1885-1925, Op. Cit. P.84
41. Bray, John : 'Christianity in Ladakh: 1920-56, Op.Cit.P.212
42. Ibid.
43. Rizvi, Janet: 'Ladakh : Crossroads of High Asia', Delhi, Oxford Univ. press, 1983 P. 197
44. Wessels, C. 'Early Jesuit Travellers in Central Asia', Delhi, Book Faith India, 1998, P. 38
45. Guge had been part of the Ladakhi empire and was later allotted to one of the Younger sons of Nyima-Gon, the founder of the Ladakhi dynasty. In 17th Century Guge became an independent Kingdom. Cf. Janet Rizvi, Op.Cit. P. 197
46. Sykes, Percy : 'A History of Exploration', London, Rontledge & Kegan Paul, 1934 P. 161
47. Rizvi, Janet:, Op.Cit.P.199
48. Jina, Prem Singh:, Op. Cit.P.15
49. Wessels,C:, Op.Cit.PP.82-83
50. Ibid, PP.76-99 & Janet Rizvi, Op.Cit.P.201
51. From a letter of Fr. Desideri translated from a French translation of the same by Du Halde, In: Letters Edifiantes, Vol.XV, P.184, See Appendix-I in Clements R.Markhan, 'Narratives of the Mission of George Bogle to Tibet and of the Journey of Thomas Manning to Lhasa; Op.Cit P.302
52. Ibid, PP.304-305
53. As found in a letter of Desideri from Leh on 5th August, 1715 addressed to the General of the Society of Jesus in Rome; as quoted by Graham Sandberg, 'Exploration of Tibet : History and Particulars, Delhi-1973-P.53
54. From a letter of Desideri, See Chements R. Markhan, Op.Cit. P. 306.
55. Wessels, C.: Op.Cit.P.179
56. Fr. Herbert 'Vanghan founded St. Joseph's Society of Foreign Mission of which the first Mother House was in Mill Hill, London and therefore the society is known after the name of the place as the Mill Hill Mission.

    Cf. Ronney, John: 'On Rocky Ground: The Catholic Church in the North-West Territories, Rawalpindi, Christian Study Centre, 1987, P.34
57. Ibid, PP.41-43

58. Ibid, P.43
59. Bray, John: 'The Roman Catholic Mission in Ladakh'. In: Recent Research on Ladakh, Proceed of the Sixth International Colloguium on Ladakh: Motilal Pub New Delhi, 1997, PP.32-33
60. Illustrated Catholic Mission, 6 (1891-92), PP. 86-87
61. Bray, John : 'Roman Catholic Mission in Ladakh, Op.Cit.P.39

Chapter - II
HISTORY OF BUDDHISM IN LADAKH

Prem Singh Jina

Ladakh is the region of ancient civilization. Since early centuries many tribes from Central Asia and Indian plains migrated to this region. Some of them even settled down in the latter countries along the different banks of Indus river. Mon tribes, perhaps the first who migrated from India via Kullu[1] or Manali[2] to Ladakh. They came here hundreds year before the Christian era. Thus through them early civilization begin in Ladakh. Of course before them many other tribes used to come in the differents parts of Ladakh insearch of pasture grounds, but they never settled down.

Mons and Buddhism

Although there is no any such authentic records available which prove that Mons were Buddhist, yet through the activities of Buddhist missionaries who came in Ladakh during 3rd Century B.C. influenced them by Buddhism, as they had established colonies in Zangskar[3] and some parts of Ladakh. According to Francke they had colonies up to Ruthog (or Rudok), popularly known as Mongol.[4] This indicates that Mons were well civilized people and had sufficient hold in Ladakh.

Dards in Ladakh

Dards were the another Indo-Aryan tribes probably migrated in Ladakh via Afghanistan, Gilgit etc. just after Mons. They settled down in Dras,[5] and Khalatse[6] areas. When they established their colonies, hostile activities between Mons and Dards started. As a result Mons subdued and got lower status in the Dard society. Subsequently Dards started marching towards upper Ladakh. In the meantime Mons did not bear insult in the Dard Society and migrated towards Zangskar and other remote parts of Ladakh.

By the end of 5th Century A.D. Dards had their colonies in and around Leh. And Ladakh was popularly known about their name as Darel.[7] Gradually Dards made Leh as their Capital and all their ministers or royal families started living in this town. Francke found some Dard graves near Leh belonged to Dard's royal families, as they were buried in a especial manner – that after the death of minister his flesh and bones were mixed with gold powder, they then put it into vase for burial. In this connection Francke referred "Empire of the Eastern Women" and said :

"When a person of high rank dies, they strip off the skin, and put the flesh and bones mixed with gold powder into a vase, and then bury it----. At the burial of sovereign, several tens of the great ministers and relatives are buried at the same time."[8]

In olden days Leh was the encampment of nomads. Dards had their colonies and castles at the mountain near Leh. Francke says :

"sLes,[9] which signifies an encampment of nomads. These nomades were probably in the habit of visiting the Leh valley at a time when it had begun to be irrigated by Dard colonizes. Thus, the most ancient part of the ruins on the top of the rNam-rgyal,-rtse-mo[10] hill at Leh are called a Brog-pai-mkhar[12].

Francke also found some more graves which were different then the earlier near Leh Describing about these he says:

"The ancient Dard grave near the Commissioner's compound in the Leh valley had done some excavation work in 1903. The roof of the grave is more than a yard below the present level of the ground. It consists of large unknown stones of rectangular shape, each about 1.5 yards long, and a foot or so broad. The walls of the grave consists of masonry of unknown stones. It is about two yards long 1.5 yards broad, and at least six feet deep. We had not yet reached the bottom, when we stopped above the ground. Later on, the deposits accumulated and buried it but destruction did not set in. I suppose the Leh graves originally contained wooden boards, the grave contained clay pots of various sizes, a few entire, but most of them in fragments. The largest pot may have had a height of three feet, and its diameter was probably not much less. The smaller pots, which were rarer than the large ones, had a height of 10 to 15 cm there were also small, saucer - like vessels of clay, probably lamps. The pottery of the grave is not wheel - made but hand-made and characterised by very small handles. There were linear ornament impressed on several of them. Most of the pots were filled with human bones. This circumstance seems to indicates that the ancient inhabitants of the Leh valley indulged in the gruesome practice of cutting the corpses to pieces and filling clay pots with fragments. There were, it appears, between fifteen and twenty skulls in one single grave. When we opened a grave in 1903, Dr. Shawe carried home three of the skulls and took measurement of them along the antero-posterior and longest transverse diameter of the roof of the skull are (approximately) 6¾ × 5 inches, 6¾ × 5¼ inches, and 6¾ × 5¼ inches. I venture to state that all the skulls were most distinctly dolichocephalic characteristic mark of the Dards of Da, Hanu and other Dard places of Ladakh."[13]

As said earlier Dards were brave and having skill in hunting animals. Therefore, they moved out even Nyoma, Phuga etc. insearch of wild animals. And settled down along the fertile lands. Francke remarks :

"As the word aBrog-pa[14] is never used here at Nyoma,[15] nor in Rubshu,[16] to signify the pre-Tibetan inhabitants of the country I believe that the word Mon, which is here always used for them, refers to the Dard settlers of Rubshu and Nyoma district. At any rate, the Dards of Da[17] state expressly in one of their songs that they once colonised Rong-chu-rgyud,[18] which is the site of the present village of Nyoma and surroundings. But the Dard civilisation apparently went beyond the present Tibetan boundary."[19]

Thus hunting was very much popular among Dards. When they hunt any wild animal, all gathered at one place and celebrate this event like festival and if failed to do so, all again gathered at one place and expressed their grief. In both events they expressed their feelings by carvings in different ways on boulders.[20]

Similarly there was a tradition in the Dards society to exchang presents of 'flour ibex' in every auspicious occasions. Sometimes they even sacrificed goats in place of ibex. This indicates that Dards believed that ibex and goat have pure spirits. Therefore, they put their horns near graves. Francke says :

"Besides human skulls a head of a sheep, and a horn of an ox were found in the (Dard) grave. These are apparently remains of a sacrifice, or gifts to the dead."[21]

The ethnology and archaeological study of Ladakh lead to this conclusion that early settlers of Dards were more or less inclined towards natural power and considered Air, Land, Sun, Moon, Water, animals etc. as their gods or goddess.

Dards and Buddhism

During 3rd Century B.C. and thereafter many Buddhist missionaries passed through Ladakh to Central Asian countries in the propagation of Buddhism. They came in Ladakh, preached Dards about Buddha teachings, who latter influenced by Buddhism.

Ladakh during Buddha

So far as Buddhism in Ladakh is concerned, I have tried to find out the position of Buddhism in the early tribal societies of Ladakh. But it would be wished to study step by step. So, to know the details about Buddhism we have to start from the period of Buddha. As we know Buddha's first admonition to the bikkhus or monks was to go forth into the world Oh! Bikkus, he exhorted, go forth now and wander from place to place, for the gain of the many, for the welfare of the many, out of compassion for the world, for the good, for the benefit and for the well being. Possibly some Arhats[22] came in Ladakh after Buddha's preaching to monks. But it is not known whether they were able to convince the Nagas[23] who were then staying in big lakes of Ladakh.

Buddhism during King As'oka Period

It is well known fact that Buddhism received a new impetus during 3rd Century B.C. As such the third Buddhist Council was concerned at Pātaliputra and at the end of the deliberations of the Council decided to despatch missionaries under the leadership of different Buddhist scholars to disseminate Buddhism in the remote parts of his kingdom and abroad.[24] Possibly some of them visited Ladakh, as the following facts indicate the reality that As'oka ruled over Ladakh and Buddhism had its roots in this region too.

(i) According to the *Mahāvaṃsa* and the *Dīpavaṃsa* people of Himalayan land and Kashmir were converted into Buddhism. The Himalayan land then known *Himavantapadesa* which comprised Himachal Pradesh, Kashmir and Ladakh.[25]

(ii) Moggliputra Tissa[26] deputed majjhātika[27] under the direction of Emperor As'oka to propogate Buddhism in Kashmir and its neighbouring areas.

(iii) Many stupas were constructed in Sumda[28] and Tiri[29] villages, and one Buddhist temple was being constructed in the Suru valley[30] during As'oka period.[31]

Buddhism during Kuṣhāṇa period

During 2nd Century A.D. Kushana kings appeared to have strong hold in Kashmir and its neighbouring regions. Buddhism was then flourishing very well. The fourth legendary Buddhist Council[32] was held at Jalandhara[33] in Kashmir under the supervision of king Kaniṣhka[34]. After the Council Buddhist missionaries were being sent to the neighbouring countries to propogate Buddhism. Many kharōsthi inscriptions have been discovered near kha-la-tse bridge belong to kuṣhāṇa empire. As such from these inscriptions we can understand that *Vima kadhpise*, the predecessor of Kaniṣhka had political control over Ladakh. Moreover King Kaniṣhka ruled over Ladakh,[35] and constructed one chorten[36] in Zangskar called *kanika*. Thus responsible to strengthen Buddhism in the Indus Valley with the areas of Drās,[37] Suru and Zangskar.[38]

Hiuen-tsiang informed that during Emperor Kaniṣhka *Sarvāstivāda* school was flourishing very well in his kingdom. It was also propogated upto Ladakh. As such vast Buddhist literature viz. *Mahavihbāṣas* of *Sarvāstivāda* was being produced in Kashmir.[39]

However, we can not deny to this fact that Kashmir was the centre of many Buddhist scholars.[40] Among them Nagarjuna[41] was a famous scholar and the founder of *Madhyamika* philosophy. According to Kalhaṇa Acharya Nagarjuna was learned Buddhist scholar, because of his presence in Kashmir, Buddhists followed non-interfering policy, and all together devoted themself in the propogation of Buddhism. Nagarjuna defeated in arguments the Pandits who uphold the worship of Shiva. Thus influenced Kaniṣhka, who latter helped Buddhism and spread it throughout in his kingdom including Ladakh.[42]

Buddhism during Fa-Hsien

During fourth Century A.D. *Sarvāstivāda* school flourished in Patliputra[43] as well as in China.[44] China also had many Buddhist Centres like India. The cultural and spiritual relation between two countries were fruitful, annually Buddhist scholars of both countries visited to India and vice-versa. Under this relationship Fa-Hsien, a Chinese monk and Buddhist scholar came India during early fifth Century A.D.; while travelling towards Kashmir he passed through the Bolor Tagh range and later acknowledged that just at the frontier of Bolor Tagh range a small country called *Darel*.[45] He saw many priests of Lesser Vehcile[46] in this country. Upasak remarks :

"In this country, *Darel*, there was a *Lo-han*[47] who, using his divine power carried a clever artisan to go the *Tusita*[48] to observe the heigh, complexion and features of Bodhisattva Maitreya. He made such three journeys and afterwards executed an image of Maitreya in wood of 80 feet high, the folded legs measuring eight across."[49]

The above statement seems to be correct as I have seen Maitreya images on wood in Sumda village of Ladakh.

Thus keeping in view the above facts, I may say that Ladakh was influenced by Buddhist missionaries, during fourth Century A.D. when Fa-Hsien visited Ladakh region.

Hiuen-tsian and Buddhism

Hiuen-tsiang was a famous Chinese pilgrim, came in India during 630 A.D. Probably he had followed the same route of Fa-Hsien. Like Fa-Hsien he also came across to *Darel*. According to him this country, located in the middle of high Himalaya passes, looked like *Udyāna*.[50] Upasak says :

"Hiuen-tsiang, another Chinese pilgrim who came in this area (Ladakh) in about 630 A.D. He called this country *Darel*. He further observes that to the north of the city *Mungoli*, crossing many mountains and defiles, sometimes passing across the iron chains and sometimes over flying bridges, going a thousand *li* or so, he came to the valley of *Ta-li-lo* or *Darel*, identical with the old capital of *Li-chang-na i.e. Udyāna*. In this valley there is a large *Saṅghārāma*, by tne side of which is carved wooden statue of Maitreya Buddhisattva, of golden colour and very majestic in appearance."[51]

Hiuen-tsiang when passed through Ladakh he got an experience that Ladakh being influenced by *Hīnāyana*. So, he did not pay much of his attention on it, as he was a monk of *Māhāyana school*. Upasak says :

"It may also be mentioned here that Hiuen-tsiang in his account pays little attention to the *Hīnāyana school* as he was a *Māhānaya* monk. He often passes without giving any comment about the *Hīnāyana school* of Buddhism. It appears feasible that by the time when Hiuen-tsiang visited this area, *Hīnāyana* Buddhism was prevalent."[52]

Downfall of Buddhism in Srinagar and its impact on Ladakh

After the death of Kaniṣhka, Buddhism received a great setback. The native dynasty of Kritya then ruled Kashmir and became the persecutor of Buddhism. Abhimanu restored the Naga cult. When Nagarjuna went to Southern India, Nora – the another Kritya king destroyed Buddhist temple and burnt viharas. King Mihirukula also a powerful persecutor of Buddhist institutions during sixth Century A.D. But they were unable to destroy Buddhism completely. Thereafter Jayendra patronized Buddhism and then Yuddhistra II's minister strengthened it by constructing *Vihāra*[53] and *Chaityas*[54]. During Ranaditya period it once again enjoyed royal respect. In the 7th Century Buddha was regarded as an incarnation of Vishnu and his images were worshipped. After Vikramaditya, Durlabhavardana ruled over Kashmir for thirty six years, he also had soft corner for Buddhism. During his reign Hiuen-tsiang visited Kashmir and noticed that both *Hīnāyana* and *Māhāyana* lived together in peaceful manner. Thus during this period though Buddhism was not given patronage by any Hindu King in Kashmir, it was having very good position in valley as well as in its neighbouring areas, there were above one hundred monasteries, five thousand Buddhist priests and other related Buddhist institutions in the valley.[55] During this period several Buddhist images made on rocks in the different parts of Ladakh. Popular among them is a carving of future Buddha of 200 metre high crag at Mulbe.[56] This colossal figure of Maitreya modelled on older *Gāndāra* type.[57]

During 8th Century Tantric form of Budhism developed in Kashmir. But Vishnuism and Shivaism had strong grip in the valley. And by the end of tenth Century they became so powerful that Buddhism completely lost its royal faith. Moreover, further revival had taken place during 11th Century; many *Vihāra* thereafter being constructed viz. Navamath, Sullā, Cankuna, Bijā etc. And till 12th Century it was flourishing well, but after the Islamic pressure Buddhism did not able to survive in valley.

In brief the causes of the downfall of Buddhism in Kashmir valley can be summerized as under :

(i) First set back to Buddhism occurred in valley when king Mihirukula destroyed thousands Buddhist monuments and Buddhist monks were unable to follow Buddhist Vinaya rules.

(ii) Buddhists became corrupt during 8th Century and failed to get faith of Hindu Kings in the valley.

(iii) Monks and Nuns lost their morality in 10th Century. In the meanwhile Hindu preachers viz. Kumarila Bhatt, Shankarachārya and Abhinavgupta were able to get public faith and helped to uproot Buddhism from the valley.

(iv) In the middle of 14th Century Shah Mirza became the King of Kashmir, he disregarded Buddhism. Thereafter King Haider Shah and Sikander immerged as terrors for Buddhism and Hinduism.

> They completely destroyed Hindu and Buddhist monuments and killed thousands Hindu and Buddhist priests.[58]

Though Buddhism lost its faith in Kashmir valley, it was undoubtedly flourishing very well in Tibet. Ladakh, therefore, turned towards Tibet and established cultural and spiritual relations with the Tibetan Govt. as well with the Tibetan monasteries.

Buddhism in Tibet and its relations with Ladakh

The introduction of Buddhism into Tibet can be noticed as early as in the 3rd Century B.C. when Emperor As'oka sent Buddhist missionaries there in the propogation of Buddhism. According to the legends and stories prevalent in Tibet indicate that Tibet had constant contact with Buddhist mission in the fourth Century A.D. These are some earlier sources of Buddhism in Tibet. But through these it is not confirmed that Tibetan were the followers of Buddhism. However, the definit evidence about Buddhism in Tibet can be traced from 7th Century when Srong-btsan-gam-po[59] was the king of Tibet. He married with two princesses— one from Nepal[60] and another from China.[61] These two queens persuaded Srong-btsan-gam-po to introduce Buddhism in Tibet.[62]

When Srong-btsan-gam-po came in power he noticed that Buddhism had no importance in his Kingdom, it felt him great. Therefore, he decided to give his full support in the propogation of Buddhism in Tibet. But again there was language problem, as there was no written language in Tibet. Thereafter, for the establishment of Buddhism he sent Sambhuta[63] with sixteen companions to Kashmir to learn Sanskrit language and compose such language in which Buddhist texts from Sanskrit can be translated. Sambhuta went to Kashmir. He studied Sanskrit language, after returning from Kashmir he composed grammar for Tibetan language. King Srong-btsan-gam-po then order his intelligent people to learn Tibetan language and help in the translation work. He, in this way first time laid the foundation of Buddhism in Tibet. Many books from Sanskrit were then translated in Tibetan language for public benefit. He also asked his subject to observe the following moral values.[64]

(i) To have faith is Kon chhog (god).

(ii) The performance of religions observance and study.

(iii) To honour one's parents.

(iv) To respect the meritorions and to promote the talented.

(v) To honour the elders as well as those who are of high birth etc.

(vi) To pay attention to relatives and friends.
(vii) To be patriotic and useful to one's own country.
(viii) To be honest and upright.
(ix) To know the good use of food and wealth.
(x) To follow the example of the good.
(xi) To be grateful and return the kindness of benefactors.
(xii) to use just weights and measures.
(xiii) To be free from jealously by establishing concord and harmony with all.
(xiv) Not to listen to the words of women.
(xv) To be gentle and polite in speech and acquire skill in conversation.
(xvi) To bear suffering and distress with patience and meekness.

In order to promote peace and harmony King Srong-btsan-gam-po himself followed the above moral virtues, so that his subjects may follow these accordingly. Besides he procured for himself a self-created image of chenressig[65] with eleven faces made of Nagas-sara sandal wood and got initiations of Arya Avalokitesvara; his two queens also regarded as the incarnations of Tara.

Srong-btan-gam-pa was the first King in Tibet who gave patronage to Buddhism. He erected one hundred and eight temples. The two great temples viz. *Ram-chha* and *Lhasa-Prul-man-ki-Tsug-la-khan*, he dedicated to the two images of Aksobhya and Sakya respectively. In 642 A.D. he sent his ministers to north China to erect 108 *chapels* at *Re-vo-tse-ma*. To propogate Buddhism in grass root level he invited great Pandits from India, Nepal and China; popular among them were Pandits *Kusara*,[66] *Sankara Brahmama*,[67] *Sila Manju*[68] and *Hwa-shan-Maha-tse*,[69] with the help of these Pandits he asked Tibetan scholars to translate original Buddhist texts from Sanskrit and Chinese into Tibetan language. Among Tibetan scholars who were engaged in the translation work were : *Sambhuta* and *Lha-lun-dorje-pal*.

King Srong-btan-gam-po devoted his better period fully in religious work. He constructed many religious edifices and sacred images, and organized a regular service by translating books on rites and ceremonies and in 650 A.D. he passed away from the world. After Srong-btsan-gam-po, there is little information about Buddhism in Tibet for some decades.[70]

In 734 A.D. Thi-Sron-de-tsan[71] became the King of Tibet. He had great inclination for Buddhism. He invited *Santaraksita*[72] and Pandit *Padma Sambhava*[73] from *Udyāna* for the propogation of Buddhism in Tibet. King Thi-Sron-de-tsan gave his full assistance to *Santaraksita* and *Padma Sambhava* in their work in Tibet. Many *Sutra* and *Tantra* were translated and inumerable religious symbols such as images of Buddha and saints and *chortens*[75] were being constructed. Not only this they concealed many sacred treasures for the benefit of future generations. *Padma Sambhava* founded the great monastery *Samye*.[76]

During Thi-Sron-de-tsan's reign one Chinese sage, *Hwashan Mahayana*[77] arrived in Tibet. He made strange theories of Buddhism which created confusion among public. Thereafter to remove the fallacious theories of *Hwanshan Mahayana* King invited Pandit *Kamalasila*[78] from India. After a long discussion *Kamalasila* defeated him. Thereafter King put down the Bon religion and persecuted all unbelievers in Buddhism and helped to strength Buddhism in his Kingdom.[79] Later after a prosperous regime of 46 years, at the age of 59, King Thi-Sron-de-tsan passed away.

After Thi-Sron-de-tsan, his eldest son Muni-tsanpo[80] came into the throne. Like his father he also assisted Buddhist scholars to spread Buddhism. He made large offerings to the great monastery of *Samye* and distributed alms to the indigent and helpless.[81] But his mother did not like his activities of helping poors, so she gave him poison and crown her youngest son Mutig-tsanpo.[82] He received lessons on Buddhism from *Padma Sambhava*, thereafter he ordered Tibetan scholars to translate original Buddhist texts from Sanskrit into Tibetan. In addition to this he built Dorje-Vyin temple at Gyal-de-kar-chum. He was strong follower of Buddhism and strenuously exerted himself to promote the welfare and happiness of his people.

Thereafter Ralpachen[83] became the King of Tibet. Immediately after becoming the King he sent offerings to the different temples. Like his ancestors he inclined towards Buddhism and wholeheartedly devoted himself in the propogation of Buddhism and invited many scholars from India, popular among them were *Jina Mitra, Surendra Bodhi, Silendra Bodhi, Dana Sila* and *Bodhi Mitra* with the help of these scholars Tibetan scholars translated many original Buddhist texts into Tibetan; popular among them were : *Ratna Rakstia, Manjusri Verma, Dharma Raksita, Jina Sena, Ratnendra Sila, Jaya Raksita, Kawapal-tseg* (*kavadpal bTsegs*), *Chodo-Gyal-tshal* (*chogror-Gyal-mtshan*) *etc*.

King Ralpachan organized many classes of priesthood and assigned revenue for monks, through which he was always ready to fulfil the basic needs of monks.[84]

Thus it is easy to understand that during the first phase (i.e. from King Srong-btsan-gam-po to Ralpachen), Buddhism was introduced in Tibet, latter it was gradually propogated throughout in Tibet (fig. 2.1). Srong-btsan-gam-po founded *Nying-ma*[85] sect which latter spread in Tibet as well in the neighbouring regions with the kind support of *Padma Sambhava*. Naturally during 8th Century A.D. *Padma Sambhava* came in Ladakh and founded *Nying-ma* sect. During the course of his visit to Ladakh he meditated different places in Ladakh. Here follows some of them.

1. **Place near Gurduwara :** It is said that *Padma Sambhava* came near Leh and met Ge-lam kesar[86] above Nimo village. Both conveyed their good wishes to each other in their works. At present one can see spring water at this place.
2. **Tak-Thog Gonpa :** This gonpa is situated about 50 km. from Leh towards East. This is the only monastery belonging to the *Nying-ma* order. *Padma Sambhava* also known Guru Rin-po-che is said to have founded this monastery. The temple where he meditated is still to be seen at Tak-Thog monestery. The monastery is tucked in the lap of a rock and owes its name to its roof which is a natural rock. Tu-Phuk houses the images of Guru-Tsan-gyet.[87]

   There are four caves in Sakti[88] called Garche-Phak, Kyit Phuk, Padma Phuk and Khandu Phuk. Here on the rock one can still see *Padma Sambhava's* body imprint like his foot, hand etc. It is said *Padma Sambhava* meditated one of the above came on his journey to Tibet.
3. **Sani :** This picturesque village is 6 kms west of Padum,[89] on the road to Kargil.[90] The chief attraction here is the castle-like monastery, which unlike other monasteries of the region is built on level ground.[91] It is said that *Padma Sambhava* sat near the Kanika chorten and meditated for five years, during the course of meditation he kept his back towards kanika chorten. After meditation he name this place *Mahagyalila Marghat.*[92] According to Ladakh chronical *Padma Sambhava* suppressed the demons.[93]

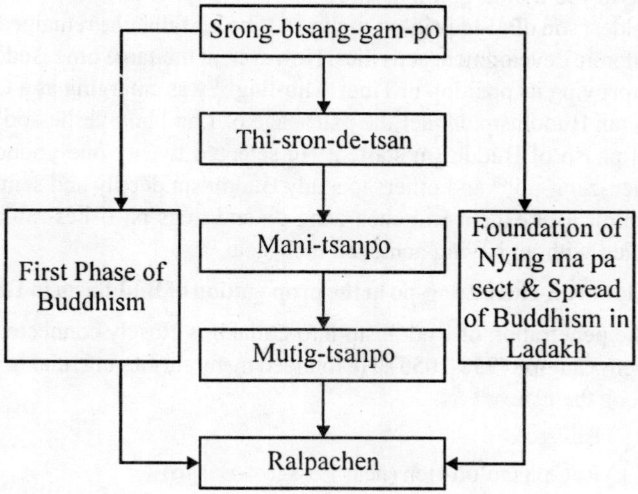

Fig. 2.1 : Development of Buddhism and its influence in Ladakh

Buddhism in Ladakh During Mid 8th Century

As said earlier during this period Buddhism was flourishing very well because of the following reasons :

(i) King Thi-Sron-de-tsen had given his full support to the Buddhist scholars in the propogation of Buddhism.

(ii) Acharya Padma Sambhava successfully suppressed demons and evil spirits.

Therefore, coitnessing the successful operations of Buddhist scholars over demons, the merchants and renowned persons of Ladakh also helped in the propogation of Buddhism in Ladakh.Perhaps in this connection they invited, Kashmiri artists from Kashmir. The Kashmiri artists would also feel that their position in Kashmir is not good, therefore, they accepted the offer and latter made rock and wood sculptures. Popular among rock sculptures called— Mulbe and kartse; However, one can find juniper wooden statues called *shid-kyi-bDag-Po* in Ladakh.[94]

Buddhism in Ladakh during 9th to 11th Century

Skyid-lde-nyima-gon[95] was the first king of Ladakh during 9th Century. He inclined to Buddhism and ordered the principle sculptures at

Sheh[96] which is popularly known *Sman la.*[97]

Skyid-lde-nyima-gon had three sons.[98] He gave Ladakh[99] Kingdom to his eldest son dPal-lde-rig-pa-mgon.[100] Like his father he remained busy in Economic development activities. However, at the same time Buddhism was improving its position in Tibet. Tho-ling[101] was emerging as a Centre of Tibetan Buddhism. Under the patronage of Lha-lama-yeshes-od[102] the second phase of Buddhism started. He selected twenty one youngmen, Rin-chen-zang-po[103] and others to study Buddhism deeply and sent them to Kashmir. But except Rin-chen-zang-po and Legs-pa'i-shes-rab all of them died without having achieved their goal.[104]

The role of Rin-chen-Zang-po in the propogation of Buddhism in Ladakh

The penetration of Buddhism into Ladakh is closely connected with Rin-chen-Zang-po (958-1055). He founded many shrines in Ladakh, popular among them are:[105]

(i) Ba-sgo
(ii) Rag-pa mc'od-rten (near Ba-sgo = Basgo)
(iii) two reuined mc'od-rten (chorten) near Sa-spo-la (Saspol)
(iv) Man-rgyu monastery
(v) A little chapel at Mul-bhe (= Mulbec)
(vi) Myar-ma (= Ṅar-ma)
(vii) A-lci (= Alchi) : The real founder was bskal-ldan-śes-rub
(viii) dPe-t'ub (spituk)
(ix) Nye temple
(x) Chorten at Kyungam village in Rong-chanthang
(xi) Mani Sarmo of Leh
(xii) Gser-khi-mchod-rten-mgo-lnga at Saki
(xiii) Chigtan
(xiv) Seṅ-ge-sgaṅ (Singh-ge-gang) at Lamayuru monastery
(xv) gSum-da
(xvi) Te-ri
(xvii) Wan-la
(xviii) A-ti-tse
(xix) Man-rgya
(xx) Gyun-drum
(xxi) Dnul-hbye-dpal-ldan-rtse
(xxii) Sa-bu-tar-chud (or Thar-rgyun-lha-khan)

(xxiii) Sle-lha-khan-gsum-risegs

(xxiv) Sle-Chos-Khor

(xxv) Nar-Chun

(xxvi) bKra-shis-sgan

(xxvii) dBen-sa

(xxviii) Mgar-bo-gron

(xxix) kyi-li-bug

(xxx) Sgan-las chos khor near Leh

(xxxi) White temple of Hunder (Nubra)

(xxxii) Red temple of Hunder (Nubra)

(xxxiii) Lha-bran of d'Tar-kha

It is therefore, Rin-chen-Zang-po's great contribution that Buddhism came into the taking up stage in Ladakh. He visited Kashmir on two occasions.[106] In Kashmir he studied Buddhism under learned Buddhist scholars viz. *Yogi Ratnasiddhi, Pandit Gunamitra, Dharmashantra, Shraddakaravarman, Boddhashri, Naropa, Pandit Kamalagupta,* etc. Thereafter he translated 161 works. These include eighteen treatise on the Sutra and tantra of Kangyur, thirty-three works of commentary on Sutra and 110 treatise of commentary of tantras. Among these, fourteen works were exclusively translated by him and, rest 147 works, he collaborated with other lochavas and Indian translators, some of them are : *Dipankara Shrijnana Atisha, Shraddakaravarman, Padmakaravarman, Subhashita, Kamalagupta, Dharmashribhadra, Lochava Tashul-Khrims-you-tan, Projnashrigupta, Viryabhadra, Tathagatasakshita, Lochava Shes-rab-legs-pa, Lochava Shakya-blo, Prajnakaravarman, Gangadhara, Buddhabhadra, Janaradana, Buddhashrishanti, Vijayashridhara, Devakara, Kanakavarman* etc.[107]

Temples Contemporary with Rin-chin-Zang-po

When we talk about the contribution of Rin-chen-Zang-po in the development of Buddhism in Ladakh, there are many temples which are equally important in the propogation of Buddhism. These temples were built during 11th Century A.D. Some of them are as follows :[108]

1. Sani gompa (before restoration)
2. Ruins east of Basgo (in Leh district)
3. Rgya-mtsha ruins north of Leh
4. Mun-dig-lha-khang ruin in the mkhar-bu (kharbu)

5. Lha-khang-gog-po ruins of Wa-kha (Wakha)
6. Ruins of chigtan Lha-Khang

From the above details we understand that Rin-chen-Zang-po wholly dedicated his services in the propogation of Buddhism. His most productive period was between 989-999 A.D., when he not only founded temples and chos-khors, but also headed the whole establishment of scholars and translators. In a way I may say Rin-chen-Zang-po's herculean task in a small span of ten years definitely paved new tradition of decorating monasteries by paintings.[109]

Naropa and Buddhism

Rin-chen-Zang-po met the great Buddhist tantric scholar and Siddha, Naropa (956-1040 A.D.)[110] at the latter's retreat at Phullahari in the northern Kashmir and received instructions on meditation on mahamudra. He visited Ladakh and blessed the present side of Lamayuru monastery.[111] This monastery claims to be the oldest monastery in Ladakh. The oldest building here called Sen-ge-sgaṅ (or Singh-ge-gang) is attributed to Lochava[112] Rin-chen-zang-po.[113]

Naropa spent sometime in Zongkhul monastery in Zangskar.[114] The two caves around which the present monastery has developed are said to have been used by Naropa for solitary meditation. A foot print on a stone near the ingress of the lower cave is reserved as that of the yogi.[115]

Atisa and Buddhism

After Lha-lama-yeshes-od, his grandnephew Byang-chub-'od[116] ordained monk and responsible for inriching Buddhism as he acquired great proficiency in Buddhism and in heretical philosophies and was very much attached to the great translator. He personally took great interest in Buddhism and was very much interested in the restoration of Buddhism, he thought greatly to invite an eminent Indian Pandit who could be profoundly versed in all the Sastras and particularly qualified in the three branches of Buddhism, viz. theory of meditation, practice and observance, beside possessing a thorough acquaintance with the five Buddhist learnings. In order to search such scholar he sent emissaries to India. Latter he was informed about a great Buddhist scholar Atisa. The King became anxious to invite him to Tibet. He sent a team of his loyal men under the leadership of Negtsho Lochava. He sent large quantities of gold and other valuable presents through his envoys to Pandit Atisa. After reaching the city of Vikramasila, then the headquarter of Aryavarata and the residence of Pandit Atisa, King's envoys offered present and requested him to visit Tibet as Buddhism was reviving in their mother country. Therefore, under such circumstance, Pandit Atisa role would be remarkable to strengthen Buddhism there; but last not least his presence in Tibet would difinitly help all living beings; likewise he thought many things and finally decided to quit his monastery Vikramasila. Then at the age of 59, in 1043 A.D. he arrived in Tibet and at the same time went to Tho-ling monastery. Here, he met Rin-chen-Zang-po and was very much influenced by his scholarly knowledge of Buddhism. When Rinch-chen-Zang-po called him in his meditation room, he saw Rin-chen-Zang-po's separate seats for meditating the different Buddhist deities. Then he thought that he reached here at the right time; and asked Rin-chen-Zang-po, "why do you have separate seats for meditating different deities, can you meditate all of them through one seat?" He latter advised him not to meditate deities separately, instead to meditate them at one seat. Rin-chen-Zang-po latter improved his method of meditation and according to the advise of Pandit Atisa he started meditation. Soonafter, this meditation process came in Ladakh and Buddhist scholars who believed kadampa sect, followed his method of meditation.[117]

Pandit Atisa then visited U' and Tsan, where he turned the wheel of Dharma. He wrote many useful sastras viz. *Lam-don* etc. He also instructed the king about Tantra. At the age of 73, in 1055 A.D. he died.[118]

During 11th Century A.D. because of the blessing of Pandit Atisa and Rin-chen-Zang-po's whole hearted devotion in Buddhism, Kadampa sect[119] spread in Ladakh. As a result in 1050 A.D. king Ol-de[120] founded spituk monastery[121] in Ladakh. This monastery belonged to Kadampa order and continued its function under this order till 13th Century.[122] Lochava Rin-chen-Zan-po himself visited this monastery and predicted that Buddhism would take root at spituk. Likewise kadampa order flourished in other parts of Ladakh popular among them are : Phyang, Saspol and Lamayuru. One can still finds some old remains of temples belonged to kadampa order.

Marpa and Buddhism

Like Ol-de (= hOd-de), his son Tse-de[123] inclined towards Buddhism. He assembled all lamas of U', Tsan and Kham, in this grand convocation he exhorted them to maintain the honour of Buddhism. Thereafter Marpa, Mila, Pandit Sakya Sri of Kashmir continued to carry forward the old tradition of meditation in the following year. Marpa visited Zangskar and founded Stongdey monastery.[124] Thereafter, like his guru Naropa, he established the meditation tradition in this monastery.

Buddhism during King Lha-chen-rgyul-po

Lha-chen-rgyul-po[125] was the first king during whom real Lamasery was established at Likir[126] in Ladakh. This is certainly one of the ancient monastery in Ladakh. According to Francke Likir monastery was founded by king Lha-chen-rgyal-po, he says :

"It is stated to have been founded (the Likir monastery) by Lama Lha-dbang-chos-rje and king believe that these two persons were contemporaries. King Lha-chen-rgyal-po lived in the eleventh century, and the lama is most probably identical with the famous pupil of bTsong-kha-pa (Tsoṅ-k'a-pa),[127] Lha-dbang-blo-gros-chos-rje converted the lamas to the reformed doctrines of the Ge-lug-pa (dGe-lugs-pa) order, and thus founded the monastery afresh as a Ge-lug-pa (dGu-lugs-pa) establishment."[128]

During investigation Francke found a temple below the Likir monastery about which he was informed that it was established earlier to Likir monastery and represented Srong-btsan-gam-po period. He remarks.

"Blow the monastery of Likir,[129] there is a large *mchod-rten*[130] which contains frescoes inside. They represent bTsong-kha-pa (Tsoṅ-k'a-pa) and other lama of his times. Paintèd above the door, a very strange figure is found which looks very much like one of the ordinary representations of Srong-btsan-sgam-po (or Srong-tsan-gam-po). I was told by the lamas that it represents a lama of Srong-btsan-sgam-po's times. The figure wears a three-pointed hat of white colour and carries two leopard skins under his arms. The lower part of this *mchod-rten* is a room, square in ground plan, which the lama said was the earliest temple at Likir, and was already in existence when Lha-chen-rgyal-po built the monastery."[131]

Now if we summarize the above discussion the following conclusion may be made. Sron-btsan-gam-po was the first King who founded Buddhism in Tibet in a strong manner. Thereafter Thi-Sron-de-tsan accelerate the Buddhist tradition throughout in Tibet and Ladakh with the help of Guru Padma Sambhava. In the following centuries and in particular during 10-11th centuries Lha-Lama-yeshes-od and Rin-chen-Zang-po developed Buddhism in Tibet and Ladakh. However, at the same period when territorial subdivision made by Skyid-lde-nyima-gon, it was formally declared that Tibet as Buddhist country and Kashmir a non-Buddhist country.[132] Ladakh thereafter came close to Tibet and Buddhism spread throughout in Ladakh according to Tibet monastic tradition. Then great yogis from Kashmir came in Zangskar for meditation. This tradition of meditation latter carried forward by their pupils, popular among them were Naropa, Marpa etc. Perhaps it would be possible that some Kashmiri artists also migrated at the border of Ladakh during 10-11th Century and lived there for long period. They had strong faith on Buddhism and made some sculptures of Boddhisattvas. Such sculptures of 10th century A.D. of Dras valley are justify the above statement. Francke had described about these sculptures in the following way :

1. The first stone which is the smallest, shows a man on horseback, his eight hand on the bride, and his left hand above his head, probably welding a sword. This rider represent a Rānā (*skr, rājānaka*). This stone has a very clear Śaradā inscription on the reverse.
2. The second stone is about six feet high. The carving shows a plain Maitreya. He wears a three-pointed tiara, and has a rosary in his raised right hand, and a vase in his left, three small figures, probably human devotees who reach upto his knees, are carved below him, one on his right and the two other on his left. Below them is a lotus throne which contains the figures of two lions couchant. To the left of Maitreya's head is carved another very small human figure. To the right of his head is carved a Śāradā inscription which is, however, a very dilapidated condition.
3. The third stone is also six feet high, and shows a standing human figure. The right hand is raised, and the left hand is probably carrying some object. The head-dress has been destroyed. This figure apparently represents Avalokitāśvara (or Avalokitesvara). On his right and left we see two female figure which are almost of the same size as the main image. They are represented in the "Indian attitude" resting on one foot, and holding one hand above their heads. They may be taken as representation of the two Tārās. Below the female on Maitreya's right, we see three small kneeling figures, with their hands raised in supplication (skr. *añjali*). Below Avalōkiteśvara, there is lotus throne, with two miniature figures emerging from it. There were probably also several small standing figures on both sides of Avalōkiteśvara, reaching up to his knees; but they cannot now be distinguished. On the reverse of this stone, there is a large and elaborate carving of a *stūpa*, with thirteen umbrellas on the top. There are also thirteen step below it leading up to a square in the centre which contains human figure. Above the head of the female figure to the left of Avalōkiteśvara, we discovered a much damaged inscription, partly in Tibetan. All the sculptures seem to date approximately from the 10th Century A.D.

4. The fourth sculptured stone stands on the opposite side of the road. The carving represents a full-blown lotus flower as we often find them on the fountain tablets of Manchad. But this one was decorated with additional vases on the four cardinal points of the wheel."[133]

Therefore it would be very clear that due to the disturbances in Kashmir valley many Kashmiri artists would be migrated to the border of Ladakh, latter when Rin-chen-Zang-po started the movement for constructing chodrtens and temples in Ladakh and its adjoing areas they helped him and under his instructions painted monasteries and chorters walls.

Lha-chen Utpala (or Lha-C'en-Utpala) and Ladakh

He was the son of Lha-chen-rgyal-po and ruled Ladakh about twenty five years from 1125 to 1150.[134] His main contribution was to unite all vassal chiefs under one umbrella without disturbing the activities of Buddhist monasteries in Ladakh.

Lha-chen Naglug (Lha-C'en Nag-lug)

About 1150-1216 A.D.,[135] king Lha-chen Naglug constructed two palaces viz. Wanla[136] and Kha-la-tse,[137] so that he could properly lookafter public affairs. Besides, he constructed a bridge over Indus river in kha-latse village.

Lha-chen Naglug, equally interested in the propogation of Buddhism. In 1215 he patronized 'Jig-rten-mgon-po, thus Ladakh came under the influence of Drigung-pa ('Bri-guṅ-pa) order.[138] He started a tradition to send Ladakhi novices to Tibet for higher spiritual studies. Petech says :

"It was perhaps the missionary zeal of the 'Bri-guṅ-pa that persuaded king dṄas-grub-mgon (or Nag-lug) to lay down for the first time the rule that Ladakhi novices should go to dBus and gTsoṅ for higher studies and ordinations. This rule had a baneful effect in the long run. It meant absolute spiritual dependence from Central Tibet; it hindered the rise of an original philosophic and literacy life in Ladakh; it implied the pre-eminence and spiritual overbearing of learned monks from dBus, which clashed (as even in the case) with the temporal administration of the monasteries entrusted to Ladakhi stewards (*p'yag-mdzod*)."[139]

After King Lha-chen Nag-lug to till 1250 A.D. we don't see any such development in Buddhism which would be remarkable. However, king Lhargyel[140] had done some development in this direction.

Lhargyal and Buddhism in Ladakh

About 1250-1275 A.D., a great yogi U-rgyan-pa visited Ladakh and unvailed the eight miracle rock statues in Nubra valley,[141] locally known eight gon-pos.[142] Besides, he also renovated Padma-Sambhava caves in Sakti.[143]

King Lhargyal then ordered to copy Kangyur and Stangyur in gold on indigo-tinted paper. This was the first attempt to enrich the Buddhist literature in Ladakh.[144]

King Lha-chen-jopal (dpal)

He was the son of King Lhargyal, 1275-1300 A.D. and mainly performed royal and clerical duties. He had not been attached with any major religions work.[145]

Lha-chen-ngorub and Buddhism

About 1300-1325. Like King Lha-chen Naglug, Lha-chen-ngorub ordered to send novices to Tibet. He also ordered to copy *Kangyur* (a library of 108 volumes) in two times and secret books in many times. Besides, he repaired the monastries which had been built by his aucestors and offered gold, silver, copper, coral beads, pearls, etc. to Buddha in Likir monastery.[146]

Therafter till Lha-chen-shesrab[147] no work in the field of Buddhism had been noticed. However, King Lha-chen-sherab had little attention towards Buddhism, here follows the details.

Lha-chen-shesrab and Buddhism (about 1350-75)

He built hamlet *Sengge-sgang* on the top of *Hangtsend* rock, Sabu village.[148] Besides he built *Chang* castle at the same village. He encouraged people to settle in Sabu village and follow Buddhism according to their respective monastic order.[149]

Buddhism during King Lha-chen-tri-tsug-lde

About 1375-1400, like his father Shesrab king tsug-lde was inclined towards Buddhism and built one row of chortens numbering 108 at Leh, and two such rows at Sabu.[150]

Buddhism during 15th Century in Ladakh

During this period dGe-lugs-pa order developed in Tibet. This school was founded by Tsoṅ-K'a-pa. This sect latter developed very fast throughout in Ladakh. King Grags-'bum-lde also patronized it, in 1430 Spituk[151] monastery also came under the control of this sect. Latter this monastery served as a base for the further development of this order in Ladakh.[152] Lama Lha-dbang-chos-rje was also closely associated with this and he reformed Likir monastery under dGe-lugs-pa order. Petech says :

"The fortunes of dGe-lugs-pa in Ladakh are closely connected with the activity of Lha-dbaṅ-blo-gros (Lama Lha-dbang-chos-rje). Central Tibetan texts, supported by the local tradition, attribute to him the renovation of dPe-t'ub (Spituk), which was carried out (as we have seen) reign of Grags–'bum-lde. This is unlikely because of chronological reasons and because an earlier and more authoritative source attributes it to Nam-mk'a-ba an elder contemporary of Lha-dbaṅ-blo-gros (Lama Lha-dbang-chos-rje). We find the same discrepancy in the case of Li-kyir (Likir). This old monastery was built, according to the Chronicle, in the 11th Century. For the Central Tibetan texts, it was suceeded as abbot by Lha-dbaṅ-blo-gros (Lama Lha-dbang-chos-rje)--- according to a later source, supported by the local tradition, the founder was Lha-dbaṅ-blo-gros himself."[153]

In the same period K'rig-se (Thikse) monastery was founded by sTod Śes-rab-bzaṅ-po's nephew dPal-Sés-rab-grags-pa in dGe-lugs-pa order.[154] At the north of this monastery sTod S'es-rab-bzaṅ-po founded a Chapel of the same order.[155]

According to ladakh Chronicle once King Grags-'bum-lde asked from Tsoṅ-k'a-pa that he would like to fulfil his desires to do better for his public. Then Tsoṅ-k'a-pa advised him to construct Chang-chub stupas in all four direction, which would fulfil his deisres, later king Grags-'bum-lde constructed such chortens and built Meitreya statues each in Timosgang, on the Temo hill chapal and at his palace chapal.[156] At the end of his life, Tsoṅ-k'a-pa sent two hermit monks to Ladakh. They carried a sacred image of *Amitayas* (Tse-pa-met), the Buddha of infinite life, which had been miraculously self born from the nose blood of Tsoṅ-k'a-pa.[157] The two monks presented this image to King Gras-'bum-lde; King greatly delighted, then established red temple above the main port of Spituk monastery, and gave it over to Lama Lhawang Lodors (Lha-dbaṅ-blo-gros), the first abbot of this monastery. The image of Amitayus was contained in a statue of Buddha Shakyamuni, which can now be seen in Tsogchen.[158]

Tsoṅ-k'a-pa's disciples also did a remarkable works in the propogation of dGe-lugs-pa order in Ladakh, popular among them was Shes-rab-bzang-po.[159] He founded a *gompa* at Stagmo village then he went to Zangskar and established dGe-lugs-pa order at the Karsha monastery, initially this monastery was founded by Phags-pa-shes-rab during 11th Century A.D. Shes-rab-bzang-po also visited Nubra and founded Diskit monastery there.[160]

King Grags-'bum-lde also being influenced by Sakya order. It is said that Sakya scholar Dorje Palsang after extensive travelling reached in Ladakh and at Mangtro cave meditated for some time. Later king'bum lde called him and, very much satisfied by his meditative ability and saintliness. He donated a large tract of land for the construction of Mangtro monastery of Sakya order. King helped Dorje Palsang for making the statues of Matreya, Manjushri and Vajrapani in the monastery. Besides he gave his services for wall paintings at the monastery. These paintings consist - *Dawarpal Ratna sutta and Lankavatar Suttas.*

Blo-gros-mt'og-ldan came next into the throne of Ladakh. Like his father 'bum-lde he patronized dGe-lugs-pa order, gave his full support to gSaṅ-p'u-ba Lha-dbaṅ-blo-gros and the pupil of mk'as-grub-rje. He renovated Spituk monastery and founded Stok monastery near Leh.[161]

During his reign a famous Buddhist scholar from Nubra, Pan chen Lha bSuṅ went to Tibet for higher studies in Buddhism, later he became the head of the Tashi Lhampo monastery. In later years he retuned to Ladakh and did remarkable work in the propogation of Buddhism in Upper Ladakh.[162] This shows that king encouraged monks to go to Tibet for higher studies.

It is said that King Blo gros-mt'og ldan invited Lama Lawang Lotos in Ladakh who constructed a big hall near Thikse monastery, according to local hostorians it was so big that about 1,000 lamas at a time could offer their prayers. One nunnery was also established under Thikse monastery. Besides, King ordered to built 10 heads and one thousand arms Avalokitesvara statue for Tsemo monastery at Leh and constructed one chorten in the memory of his father.[163]

In this way if we analyse the over all picture of Buddhism during 15th Century A.D. in Ladakh, at the Ist half of this Century with help of Tsoṅ-k'a-pa dGe-lugs-pa school of Buddhism spread its roots into Ladakh, soon after it became the important school of Buddhism and was getting success to convence the Kings of Ladakh such as Grags-'bum-lde, Blo-gros-mt'og-ldan etc. During the course of propogation of this sect gSaṅ-p'u-pa Lha-dbaṅ-blo-gros, mk'as-grub-rje and s'es-rab-bzaṅ-po made their valuable contribution. As a result in the middle of 15th Century head of dGe-lugs-pa sect had established many shrines in Ladakh. Later in the second half of this Century dGe-lugs-pa gained the upper hand in Ladakh, though bKa-brgyud-pa was performing very well in Central Tibet and was entering in Ladakh.

Buddhism during 16th Century in Ladakh

King Tashi Namgyal (1530-1560)[164] was a religious personality, he built Mani walls and other Buddhist shrines throughout in Ladakh. During this period 'Bri-guṅ-pa order and a sub sect of bKa-brgyud-pa was fastly reviving in Central Tibet. C'os-rje lDan-ma and the founder of sGaṅ-sṅon monastery then contributing remarkable role in the development of the 'Bri-guṅ- pa order in Tibet and its neighbouring areas. King Jamyang-Namgyal (1560-1590)[165] because of C'os-rje lDan-ma's outstanding personality invited him in Ladakh and asked him to build 'Bri-guṅ-pa order monastery. C'os-rje lDan-ma accepted King's request and founded Phyang monastery of this order. Thereafter he went Lamayuru monastery and attached it with Phyang.

King Jamyang-Namgyal was also being impressed by sTag-ts'aṅ-ras-pa (1574-1651).[166] When sTag-ts'aṅ-ras-pa was visiting to Udyana via Zangskar, King invited him to Leh, but sTag-tśan-ras-pa did not accept King's invitation and went to Udyana. It heart King's religious faith upon 'Brug-pa sect, but soon controlled himself and again turned towards religion. Then he renovated various monasteries and Buddhist shrines which were being destoyed by the Balti invasion.[167]

1. Nyilza Cave
2. Saspol Cave
3. Brag-khung-kha-bo-che at Spituk monastery
4. Lingshed monastery

Likewise when Balti Muslims destroyed the Mangtro monastery[168] King Jamyang Namgyal then with the help of Sakya lama Chokyi Lodo renovated the monastery and restored the monastic activities. Besides he devoted his latter days in the propogation of Buddhism in Ladakh and on the advise of chorje Denma (C'os-rje lDan-ma) ordered to write kargyud (bKa'-brgyud-pa) texts by golden and silver ink.

Buddhism during 17th Century

Around the end of 16th Century 'Brug-pa order became powerful and after the decline of the Tibetan power, as chinese forces occupied some of the portion of Tibet, Ladakhi King decided to become more independent in religious and political matter. In the same time when war between Bhutan and Tibet started during 1680-1683, the yellow sect[169] was again established in Ladakh.[170]

At the beginning of the 17th Century sTag-ts'aṅ-ras-pa (or Stag-tshang-ras-pa) returned from Udyana and visited Ladakh according to the promise which he made with King Jamyang-Namgyal. But when he came to Ladakh Sin-gey-rnam-gyal (Siṅ-ge-rnam-rgyal),[171] the son of Jamyang-Namgyal was the King of Ladakh. He warmly welcomed and appointed him as royal teacher of his kingdom. Thereafter with the help of his religious teacher sTag-ts'aṅ-ras-pa[172] king constructed many monasteries, some of them as under.[172]

1. Hemis (He-mis)
2. Chemre (Chem-re)
3. Wanla (Wan-le)
4. Meru (Me-ru)
5. Tashigang (sTashi-gang)

As sTag-ts'aṅ-ras-pa belonged to 'Brug-pa order, he therefore gave his full support to ascend 'Brug-pa sect. Consequently He-mis monastery received all kinds of support from the royal family. sTag-ts'aṅ-ras-pa's building activity was noteworthy, he constructed a temple and hall at Hemis. According to Petach :

"sTag-ts'aṅ-ras-pa's building activity was also noteworthy. The pet project of sTag-ts'aṅ-ras-pa was the construction of Byaṅ-c'ub-bsum-gliṅ convent at He-mis, which became and remained the royal monastery of Ladakh. At first there was a simple harmitage. Then work began in 1630 the main temple (*gtsug-lag-K'aṅ*) was built; in 1638 he was able to consecrate the great assembly (*'du-k'aṅ*), decorated with paintings."[174]

Seṅ-ge-rnam-rgyal himself looked after the religious activities, erected several-storeyed statues, silver and copper *stūpas*. At the Seljang monastery Ba-sgo he installed a huge statue of Maitreya,[175] and built Mani walls at Ba-sgo and lingshed.[176] Besides, he renovated or built a monastery of 'Brug-pa order at Nyoma. Francke says :

"I went to examine the temple which occupies the highest position in the (Nyoma) now deserted town on the rock and belongs to the a 'Brug-pa ('Brug-pa) order of monks. I was told it dated from the days of king Seng-ge-rnam-rgyal (= seṅ-ge-rnam-rgyal). The monks (showed) me proof of this assertion. They brought me a book which had been dedicated to the monastery by Seng-ge-rnam-rgyal and actually contained a dedication sheet on which the names of the king and his illustrions queen bSkal-bzang could be distinctly read. Of course, a document like that goes to prove only that Seng ge-rnam-rgyal took a certain interest in the settlement and possibly renovated the temple."[177]

The King Sen-ge-rnam-rgyal entrusted Nam-mk'a-dpal-mgon to copy several Buddhist texts, latter he was duly rewarded and given beautiful Thanka (= t'aṅ-ka). Petach says :

"One of the foremost noblemen of Seṅ-ge-rnam-rgyal's time was the lord of Sabu, Nam-mk'a'-dpal-mgon of the Mi-nag family. In the Pig year (almost 1635) the King entrusted him with the supervision of the copying of several texts (bka'-'gyur, *Aṣṭasāhasrikaprajnāpamitā*, biography of Padmasambhava, life and songs of sTag-ts'aṅ Ras-c'en), for which he was duly rewarded."[178]

After the death of Sen-ge-rnam-rgyal, his eldest son Bdel-dan Namgyal (bdel-ldan-rnam-rgyal)[179] became the King of Ldakh. He was a brave personality and was always ready to help religious works built, Sheh temple and installed three-storeyed Buddha statue. After the completion of Buddha statue he built chang-chub chorten.[180] Besides he built many Buddhist shrines, some of them are as under :[181]

1. Taire-rong Mani wall near Leh.
2. Chang-chub chortern at the one corner of Taire-rong Mani wall.
3. Namgyal chorten at the other end of Taire-rong Mani wall.
4. Avalokitesvara temple at Leh.
5. Tak-thog monastery.

King Bdelegs Namgyal[182] came on throne after the death of Bdel-dan-Namgyal. He did not contribute much for the development of Buddhism and in latter days gave equal treatment to dGe-lugs-pa as well to 'Brug-pa sect. However, King Nima-Namgyal[183] who had inherited the throne after his father Bdelegs Namgyal's death, was a religious man and inclined towards Buddhism. He ordered to bring 108 volumes of bKa-'gyur text, enriched the Buddhist tradition and constructed Mani walls and *Stupas*. Some of them are shown below :

1. Za-nag-gi Mani wall at Choglamsar.
2. A prayer wheel (Mani Tungchur) of gold, silver, and copper at Leh (Probably).
3. Images of his favourite deity, of gold and silver.

According to the Ladakh chronicle King Nima-Namgyal gave his equal regards to all monasteries. He renovated Sa-skya-pa monastery at mK'ar-rtse.[184] But under the pressure of Dalai-Lama he was bound to give more support to dGe-lugs-pa order. Petech says :

"On 28th August 1694, the regent, on behalf of the Dalai-Lama issued to him a most instresting document. It stated that, while Ladakh followed earlier the 'Brug-pa sect, now, after the conquest of dGa'-ldan-ts'e-dbaṅ its de-facto ruler (*srid-skyoṅ*) Ṅi-ma-rnam-rgyal (Nima Namgyal) showed himself obsequent to the yellow church. Therefore, the dGe-lug-pa (dGe-lugs-pa) convents of K'ri-rtse, dPe-t'ub, klu-skyil (Li-kyir), bDe-skyid, and the monasteries of the other sects, such as iCe-'dre, Aṅ-le (Wam-le), Par-brtan ('Bar-gdan in Zaṅs-dkar), Ma-rgro (Ma-spro), Gri-gu, sGaṅ-sṅon, Brag-ltag, k'yuṅ-ru, sTag-sna etc., all of them were under the authority of 'Bras-spuṅs, chief convent of dGe-lugs-pa school."[185]

Thus by and large during 17th Century 'Brug-pa ascendance was fully established by sTag-ts'aṅ-ras-pa, however, at the end of this Century dGe-lugs-pa school had started its influence in Ladakh.

Buddhism during 18th Century

In this Century Mahārsiddha Ngag-dbang Tse-ring born in Zangskar, he studied *Aṣṭasāhasrika Prajñapārmitā*, at the age of fourteen visited 'Bar-gdan monastery[186] and entered the *bhiksu-samgha* of this monastery. Latter under learned monks he studied Mahayana Philosophy of Buddhism in Hemis monastery. But returned to Zangskar for meditation at a cave of Naropa, and established meditation centre near it. During his tours to differt parts of Western Himalayas he recommended the recitation of six-syllabled *mantra Om-maṇi-padme-hūm* on all occasions. Besides preaching he promoted caltural activities. He was also responsible for the repairing works at rDzong-khul monastery,[187] painting of five Dhayāni-Buddhas and for the image of rDo-rje-'chang which he installed in the inner shrine of this monastery.[188]

Thus Eighteen Century was a revival of 'Brug-pa. During this period as 7th 'Brug-c'en dkar-brgyud - 'p'rin-las-śriṅ-rta (1718-1766) visited Ladakh.[189] Ka-thog-Rig-azin-tshe-dbang-nor-bu also started preachings and visited many areas of Ladakh, he stayed most of the time at Hemis monastery. In addition he made the following Buddhist monuments :[190]

1. Kakini chortern (*stupa*) at Meru.
2. Image of Lha rdo-rje-chen-mo for Shey (Sheh) monastery.

By the time He-mis monastery became popular throughout in Ladakh because of the presence of rgyal-bras-rinpocha Mi-pham-jam-dpal-mthu-stobs, who was the head lama of the monastery. Under his direction bzo-pa-dpal-le, the famous artist made one of the biggest Padmasambhava thanka of the world. He was the first rin-po-che who introduced the tradition of Hemis festival[191] and only once in twelve years to display the big thanka of Padmasambhava.[192]

According to Petech, Mi-pham (= Mi - p'am) also set up a lah-khang in He-mis monastery and installed some images in it. He remarks :

"(He-mis) was set up by the Mi-p'am in order to record the beginning of the construction of the He-mis *gtsug-lug-k'aṅ* in the Water-Tiger year 1782 and its completion in the Water-House year; this date corresponds either to 1762 or to 1822. At least three images of Mi-p'am are found at He-mis, all of them usually lively portraits, characterized by a white pointed beard and a half-benign and half-ironical smile. he was a patron of art;

several *t'aṅ-ka* (thanka) is in 'Ts'am-k'aṅ a great gilt *mc'od-rten* in the Bar-pa Lha-k'aṅ at He-mis made upon his order."[193]

In the meantime Tsetan Namgyal[194] showed his inclination towards the religions activities. He built the Skyin mani ringmo, the second largest mani-wall of Ladakh, with chortens at either end, of the great Namgyal and chang-chub. This mani wall is situated a littel above Deldan's mani-wall and stretches from there towards Leh.[195]

As such during 18th Century Ladakh Kings monstly involved directly or indirectly in quarrels and wars. Therefore could not pay their attention in the development of Buddhism. However, Hemis monastery remained to be the centre of religious works. The royal princes such as Saskyong Namgyal, Tsepal Namgyal etc. were donated to Hemis monastery. This indicates that Ladakh Kings gave their cash and kind support to Hemis gompa for its religious works.

Buddhism in Ladakh During 19th Century

In the beginning of 19th Century after the death of Tsetan Namgyal his brother Tsepal Namgyal who was a lama at Hemis monastery turned layman and became the king of Ladakh, but due to madness he again went to Hemis monastery for meditation. Tsepal erected many images of Buddhist deities in Ladakh, some of them are : Vajrapani with a silver head, Saint Guru Padma od bar, made of seven maunds of silver; a white Tara (sgrolma) etc. Besides he built chorten from nine maunds of silver with ornaments in gold, copper, and precious stones.[196]

In 1814 bDe-c'en-c'os-'k or Yoṅs-śes-grub-pa (1781-1845) visited Ladakh. He stayed three years in Ladakh and during this period he converted some Kashmiri Muslims to Lamas. Thereafter he returned to Tibet. After three years 8th 'Brug-c'en received invitation from the p'yag-mdzod mGon-po of Hemis, he turned down this offer.[199] However, Hemis monastery did not loose its importance for religious works.

Tsepal Namgyal's son Ts'e dbaṅ-rab-brtan-rnam-rgyal recognised as the incarnation of stag-tshang-ras-pa (sTag-ts'aṅ-ras-pa). he was known mC'og-sprul and his official residences at Hemis and lCe-'bre. On the other hand dGe-lugs-pa order also increased its activities after the downfall of Ladakhi royal dynasty in 1843. In 1860 first Bakula Rin-po-che came from Zangskar to dPe-thub (Spituk) monastery. By the third quarter of the 19th Century he founded three sub *gompas* of dPe-thub viz. Sabu, Stok and Shankar. These monasteries are situated near Leh and about 170 lamas attached with these monasteries. The present Bakula is the 20th in succession and also the head of the above monastic family.[198]

The nineteenth century was full of wars. Dogras were superior to the

Ladakhis and ruled over Ladakh. The Ladakh Empire was complely fallen down by the fast-rising power of Dogras during thirties of the 19th century. Subsequently Buddhist scholars and Rin-po-ches were unable to continue their Buddhist activities according to their plan. However, Bakula Rin-po-che did some work for the establishment of dGe-lugs-pa monasteries in Ladakh.

Buddhism during 20th Century

After the *Parinirvana* of 19th incarnation of Bakula in 1917, the 20th incarnation was born in 1919. In 1924 at the age of five years, he was installed as head of dPe-thub and bought to Shankar[199] for primary education. In 1935 he went for higher education to 'Bras-spuṅs. After getting dges-bses[200] degree he returned Ladakh and served for his monasteries. Thereafter he came in Indian politics and elected first time M.L.A. from Ladakh in the Jammu and Kashmir Assembly, later represented Member of Parliament from Ladakh.[201]

In the beginning of the 20th Century the 19th incarnation of Bakula Rin-po-che did some remarkable work in the development of Buddhism in Ladakh. As to exempt all the monasteries of Ladakh from state tax, renovate Karsha and Stongde *gompas* in Zangskar, build bla-brangs[202] in these monasteries.[203] After the *Parinirvana* of the 19th incarnated Bakula, sTag-ts'aṅ-ras-pa Rin-po-che decided to continue Buddhist activities in this region, he met Maharaja Hari Singh in Srinagar and requested him to donate a piece of land in Srinagar for the construction of a *gompa*. Maharaja accepted his request and donated land for this purpose at Raj Bagh in Srinagar.[204] This was the period when Kashmir Raj Bodh Mahasabha was established under the patronage of sTag-ts'aṅ-ras-pa Rin-po-che, latter in 1931 this organisation under the guidance of Pandit Shridhar Koul submitted the grievances to Glancy commission. After the gap of three years young Men's Buddhist Association was founded in Leh and bKa-blon Tse-sbang-rig-dzin was appointed its President. In 1950 when state government passed a bill of *Large Landed Estates Abolition Act*. Ladakhi Buddhist leaders in Ladakh reacted against it and a Buddhist delegation[205] met with Pandit Nehru in Delhi. Thereafter this delegation formed Gonpa Association to fight against the Abolition Act. Finally demonastrations against the state government were held at Leh. In 1953 a enquiry committee was appointed. Justice Jankinath Wazir was head of the committee. This Committee visited Ladakh to investigate the case of monasteries of Ladakh. In the report the committee was agreed for the possession of large land holding as the monasteries in Ladakh are religious and charitable institutions. They feed the poor and needy persons, use the agricultural products for the lamas who are residing at the monasteries and given them religions education. So lands are the only main source of income through which monastic activities servive in Ladakh. Finally when Gonpa Association convinced the Wazir committee that not to cover Ladakhi monasteries under the Estate Abolition Act, sTag-ts'aṅ-ras-pa Rin-po-che presented a site at Leh to Gonpa Association for the official use. Thereafter Bakula Rin-po-che effectively started the religious activities through Gonpa Association and requested Pt. Nehru to give full financial support to Central Institute of Buddhist studies, then a small Buddhist school. After the Indo-China war it was very difficult task for Indian government to resume the old tradition of sending lamas from Ladakh to Tibet for higher education in Buddhist philosophy. Thus he asked Pt. Nehru to develop Buddhist school as a higher learning centre of Buddhism like-Sera, Tashi-Lhampo etc. of Tibet, so that Lamas of Ladakh could get higher education in Buddhism.[206]

In 1960 Bakula Rin-po-che asked Pandit Nehru to allote site for Ladakh Buddhist Vihara and to establish a Buddhist institute in Delhi. Panditji accepted his request and presented site on the bank of the Yamuna river for Ladakh Buddhist Vihara, and established Ladakh institute for Higher studies in 1963. In this institute Buddhist students from Ladakh, Himachal and North East got admission. They were given Buddhist education with some modern Art subjects. At the same time Ladakhi Buddhists felt an urgent need to teach Bodhi language at Primary and middle schools. Bakuia Rin-po-che approached to the state government and asked them to appoint Bodhi teachers at Primary and middle schools.[207]

In 1969 for the welfare of Ladakhi youths, Lamdon Welfare Society was established in Ladakh. This Society actively started its function from 1974 and in the beginning organised Mani-dung-'phur[208] every year.[209]

Though Dalai Lama first time visited Ladakh in 1965, but in 1975 he delivered five day Kalachakra initiation at Jivetsal.[210] In 1980 via Leh he visited to Zangskar and preached Ladakhis about Buddha teachings. After the visit of Dalai Lama in Zangskar, some Buddhist monks and local resident were involved in a dispute over a portable diesel generating set brought there was a confrontation between the local population and Kashmiri Armed Police resulting in firing and injuries to 151 people. After this incident an action committee was formed under the leadership of Kushok Bakula and latter this committee demanded from the state government to allocate funds on the basis of area. The Chief Minister point out this matter seriously. Then under his direction Sikri commission appointed by the State government to inquire into the question of regional imbalances. This commission submitted its report in August 1980. On the basis the government had issued order to rectify the imbalance.[211]

In 1983 Farooq Abdullah became the Chief Minister of Jammu and Kashmir State. He put Munshi Habibullah from the Muslim-dominated Kargil district of Ladakh in his Cabinet, but there was no Buddhist in his Ministry. This created discrimination among Buddhist community in Ladakh, finally by exploiting religious sentiments and mouthing communal rhetorics. However, Dr. Farooq succeeded in affecting polarisatuion of votes on communal lines. Buddhists therefore, terribly disturbed at efforts of the government to hurt, humiliate and frustrate them on every front, including political.[212]

Conflicts and disputes in the name of religion were quite unknown. However, conversion by way of marriages with Buddhist women became quite common. And in almost all the cases Buddhist women were converted to Islam. The Buddhists remained silent, considering it a matter of personal choise, until they realised that this was being done with a definite political design and using increase their numbers in Ladakh and for that weird sense of achievement and superiority of the Buddhists.[213]

Buddhists, therefore, felt that their religion in Ladakh seems to be in danger. State government have had neglecting attitude for Buddhists and their monasteries in Ladakh. Buddhists could hardly get financial assistance for the preservation and protection of Buddhist cultural Heritage. However, on the other hand government easily provided financial assistance to Muslims and their cultural Heritage. They could get land allotments comparatively easily for Mosques than monasteries in Ladakh.[214]

Bakula Rin-po-che expressed concern over the "indifferent attitude" of the State government towards Ladakh and Buddhists in particular. He demanded for Scheduled Tribe Status to Ladakhis from the State and Central Governments. In 1986 Central government accepted this demand. A mini-census and a survey in this connection was conducted, Bodh, Balti, Drogpa, Purigpa & Mon were found ethenic groups in Ladakh. Later according to the mini-census report the central government passed on the recommendation to declare the above ethenic groups as Scheduled Tribes to State government for noticification under the State constitution. Unfortunately till the end of 1986 the state government did not consider it seriously.[215]

Thus the period between 1980 to 1986 passed in political struggle. In June 1987 Dalai Lama visited Ladakh. This time he stayed comparatevely longer period than the earlier his visits. During his 35 days stay in Ladakh he gave teaching on the Bodhisattvas charyas.[216] When Dalai Lama returned to Dharmsala in Himachal Pradesh. Buddhist leaders again thought about the descrimination attitude of State government towards Buddhists. For instance :[217]

1. Ladakh was bifurcated, purely on communal basis into mainly Buddhist populated Leh district and Shiah Muslim populated Kargil.
2. Of the four Ladakhi members in the State's Legislatve bodies three were Muslims.
3. As per a 1986 observation in Leh offices, the Muslims who were only 12% of the population occupy 39% of the jobs and Buddhist who were 86% have had only 49.79% jobs. Here follows the details :

Community-wise Government employees in different departments in Leh district.

Name of Department	Category	Buddhists	Muslims	Muslims of Kargil	Others
(1)	(2)	(3)	(4)	(5)	(6)
Animal	G.	03	01	–	08
	N.G.	25	25	03	15
Husbandry	class IV	51	49	01	–
Agriculture	G.	–	–	–	–
Deptt.	N.G.	–	–	–	–
	Class IV	69	38	–	–
Tourism	G.	01	–	–	–
Department	N.G.	06	04	06	–
	Class IV	15	14	01	–
Tehsil/Agri	G.	01	01	–	–
	N.G.	04	01	01	01
	Class IV	–	01	–	–
I.T.I.	G.	–	–	–	01
Department	N.G.	02	02	01	01
	Class IV	–	02	–	–
Cultural	G.	02	–	–	01
Academy	N.G.	06	02	01	01
	Class IV	02	01	–	–
Police	G.	–	02	–	01
Deptt.	N.G.	100	45	75	54
	Class IV	–	–	–	–

State Archieves	G.	–	–	–	–
Repository	N.G.	02	04	–	01
	Class IV	–	02	–	01
Mechnical	G.	01	01	–	–
Division, Leh	N.G.	24	19	02	19
	Class IV	13	16	01	02
District	G.	–	–	–	01
Treasury, Leh	N.G.	01	06	–	01
	Class IV	01	01	–	–
Handicraft	G.	–	01	–	–
Centre	N.G.	17	11	01	02
	Class IV	05	03	–	01
Public Work	G.	–	01	–	–
Deptt.	N.G.	12	04	–	04
	Class IV	07	–	–	–
District	G.	–	–	–	–
Library, Leh	N.G.	03	01	–	–
	Class IV	02	–	–	–
Co-operative	G.	–	–	–	–
Bank	N.G.	01	–	–	02
	Class IV	01	–	01	–
Stationary	G.	–	–	–	–
Depot	N.G.	02	–	–	–
	Class IV	–	–	–	–
Tehsil Office,	G.	–	–	01	–
Leh	N.G.	15	08	–	01
	Class IV	08	07	–	–
SICOP,	G.	–	–	–	–
Leh	N.G.	01	01	–	–
	Class IV	02	–	–	–
N.A.C	G.	–	–	–	–
Leh	N.G.	03	02	–	–
	Class IV	03	20	05	–
Electrical	G.	01	02	–	02
Div., Leh	N.G.	21	18	02	04
	Class IV	54	10	03	01
P.W.D. Circle,	G.	–	–	–	02
Leh.	N.G.	05	03	–	02
	Class IV	03	01	–	–

Civil const.	G.	01	–	–	03
Div. P.W.D.	N.G.	07	03	01	05
	Class IV	16	09	03	–
Land Develop-	G.	–	–	–	–
ment Bank	N.G.	01	–	–	01
	Class IV	–	01	–	–
Social Welfare,	G.	01	01	–	01
Leh	N.G.	06	07	–	02
	Class IV	03	04	–	–
Distt. Rural	G.	01	01	–	01
Dev. Agency,	N.G.	–	01	–	04
Leh.	Class IV	03	04	–	–
Desert Dev.	G.	–	–	–	02
Deptt.	N.G.	03	02	–	01
	Class IV	02	01	–	–
Co-operative	G.	–	–	–	–
Deptt.	N.G.	27	13	–	03
	Class IV	08	08	–	–
Fisheries	G.	01	–	–	–
Deptt.	N.G.	09	07	–	–
	Class IV	01	–	–	–
R & B. Div.	G.	–	02	01	01
Leh	N.G.	33	17	09	12
	Class IV	16	09	–	01
Employment	G.	01	–	–	–
Exchange	N.G.	01	02	–	–
	Class IV	–	01	–	–
Investigation	G.	01	–	02	–
Div.	N.G.	07	09	01	08
	Class IV	06	02	01	–
District Indus-	G.	–	02	–	02
tries, Leh	N.G.	28	25	–	04
	Class IV	07	05	–	–
Deputy Com-	G.	–	02	–	03
misioner's	N.G.	34	18	–	04
office	Class IV	10	14	–	–
Medical Deptt.	G.	18	03	–	04
(Excluding	N.G.	79	68	–	27

SNM Hospital)	Class IV	61	33	02	–
Forest Depart-	G.	01	–	–	–
ment Leh	N.G.	43	19	04	–
	Class IV	21	07	–	–
Food &	G.	–	01	–	–
Supplies, Leh	N.G.	19	14	01	–
	Class IV	18	15	–	–
Public Health	G.	–	03	–	–
Engg.	N.G.	25	15	01	26
	Class IV	03	05	–	–
Education	G.	–	03	–	05
Department	N.G.	01	01	–	–
	Class IV	04	–	–	–
Information	G.	–	01	01	–
office	N.G.	12	09	–	01
	Class IV	09	02	–	–
Igoo-Pheg	G.	01	01	–	03
Dev.	N.G.	11	17	–	10
	Class IV	14	16	06	–
A.C.T. R's	G.	01	–	–	–
office	N.G.	06	01	–	–
	Class IV	06	03	–	–
Sub-Judge	G.	–	–	–	01
	N.G.	01	01	01	01
	Class IV	02	03	–	01
Weights and	G.	–	01	–	–
Measures	N.G.	01	01	–	–
office	Class IV	–	02	01	–
Sheep Husb-	G.	01	02	–	05
andry Office.	N.G.	31	24	18	05
	Class IV	71	30	05	02

Total : Buddhist = 1198 (49.79%) Muslims = 935 (39%) and others = 273 (11.21%)

Source : Booklet on : Ladakh : People's movement for Union Territory Status; pp. 11-14.

Reviewing all the above facts Ladakhis had strong feelings that they were getting a raw deal compared to the other regions of the State — the Muslim dominated Kashmir valley and the Hindu dominated Jammu region in respect of allocation of funds and recruitment to State government service. Therefore, local Buddhist leaders demanded that Ladakh should be made a Union Territory, as the Kashmir government never liked to rise Buddhist Community in the state. The following facts indicate that how State government adopted discriminatory attitude for Ladakh and Buddhist in particular.[218]

1. Ladakh, the third most important region forming the State Jammu and Kashmir did not have a single representative in the State's 30 membered council of minister before 1988.
2. Although areawise Ladakh is for larger than both Jammu and Kashmir regions, but had only two members in the State assembly of 75 till 1988.
3. Due to the State's apathetic and unsound educational policies 95% to 98% of the student usually failed in the matriculation examination.
4. There was no facility for higher education in Ladakh and till 1988 even a single degree College was not being established.
5. The State Government had been systematically dismantled all the important forums of development such as the Ladakh affairs department in the State secretariate and the Ladakh development board.
6. Crores of rupees had been invested in the Stakna project a 4 M.W hydel project but this project proved failure in the end.

In 1989 Thupstan Chhewang became the President of Ladakh Buddhist Association, under his leadership Buddhists of Ladakh started agitation against the discrimination of Kashmir Government. The agitation was concentrated in Leh district and Buddhist dominated villages in Kargil district. The border Leh district of Ladakh finally got unrest and resulted of discontent among various committees, particularly Buddhists. Ladakhi Buddhists clashed repeatedly with Kashmir Muslims. Reports had been noticed that some Ladakhis allegedly looted and set fire to non-Ladakhi establishments. Finally when situation was beyong the control of District administration, army was called out and curfew clamped in Leh town on July 8, 1989. When the situation was brought under control and on July 12 curfew was lifted from 8 a.m to 5 p.m. total damage was estimated about Rs. 25 lakhs.[219] After the meeting with Ladakh Buddhist Association Government of India declared Ladakh region as a Tribal area and the inhabitants of this region such as Bhotos and Baltis as Scheduled Tribes. Therefore, viewing to the success of agitation Ladakh Buddhist Association further started the agitation, this time Association demanded to declare Ladakh as Autonomus Hill council status. But unfortunately this agitation converted into communal clashes. Buddhists boycott the Muslims, as a result Muslims kept themselves aside from the agition. However, Buddhists continued their agitation for the "Autonomus Hill Council to Ladakh". During the course of agitation Buddhist leaders several times met with the National Conference and Congress-I leaders in Srinagar and Delhi respectively.But in the State and Centre leadership asked them to remove the differences with Muslims and to create harmonious relations. They said "Until or unless Balti Muslims would not co-operate the agitation, the Government could not give any kind of assurance of your demands." Thus on November 29, 1992 during a tripartite talk in New Delhi, the Ladakh Buddhist Association lifted the three year old social and economic boycott against the Muslims. After this, Muslims in Ladakh agreed to cooperate with the majority in their struggle for greater autonomy, popularly known as the "Hill council status." Now the Muslims involvements in the agitation for "Hill Council Status" to Ladakh made much progress and several rounds of talks had been taken place in Jammu, Kashmir and Delhi. The Government finally agreed in principal to grant "Hill Council Status" to Leh and Kargil districts. But the Kargil delegates turned down the offer stating that they, rather wait till a proper Government would be established in the state. Then the talks being proceeded between only the delgates of Leh district and the Government. At last delegates from Leh met with Governor Mr. G.C. Saxena in January 1993 in Jammu. But this talks ended without any decision. Later Governor G.C. Saxena was replaced by Retd. General K.V. Krishna Rao, he did not pay much attention to the Ladakh issue. however, after a long gap he decided to visit Ladakh. When Ladakh Buddhist Association came to know about his visit to Ladakh, the Association immidiately sent an ultimatam to General K.V. Krishna Rao, stating that unless the Governor would ready to talk with Ladakh Buddhist Association on the issue of "Hill Council Status", the Association would not only abstain from any reception etc. but also protest his visit in Ladakh. At last Governor agreed to talk with Ladakh Buddhist

Association members in Leh. Later after the arrival of Governor in Ladakh a meeting was held in Leh with the committee. In this meeting many issues being discussed but later another dates 10th and 11th of June 1993 were fixed by State Government. A joint members team of Ladakh Buddhist Association and Ladakh Muslim Association went to Srinagar to attend the meeting. The Government side led by Chief Secretary Sheikh Ghulam Rasool while the LBA and LMA team were headed by Mr. Thupstan Chhewang and late Akbar Ladakhi respectively.[220] They discussed various issues about the structure of "Hill Council Status." But three main points remained unsolve. These were — (i) The name of the council (ii) Vice-chairman (iii) Placement of Government Employees. Besides according to the member of the Ladakh team, two important objects unfulfilled : [221]

(i) Originally it was proposed that the council budget would be presented to the State assembly for approval and the final decision in case of differences be kept with the council. This objective could not be achieved.

(ii) The second demand was that grants in aid from the Centre should be directly placed at council's diposal, without being channeled through the state Government. Although the State had no objection to this, they said that technically it was not possible.

In October 1993 tri-partite talks held in Delhi. This time delgates from Ladakh and Government side both from State and Centre team participated in the meeting. later Sh. S.B. Chavan, Union Home Minister, formally announced that the demand of "Autonomous Hill Council" would be soon considered. The State Government then made a draft of Autonomous Hill Council of Ladakh and sent it to New Delhi. This draft was received by the Law Ministry, Government of India. After thorough study of draft by the Law and Home Ministries it was sent to cabinet for formal approval before sending to President for Presidential Ordinance. Finally on May 9, 1995 President of India approved the 'Ladakh Autonomous Hill Development Councils Act'. Laying a copy of a statement on the table of the Lok Sabha, Minister of State for Home Rajesh Pilot said :

"The President of India on May 9 approved the 'Ladakh Autonomous Hill Development Councils Act'. The Act envisages at Autonomous Hill Development Council for each district of the region. Leh and Kargil, and an inter-district advisory council for the Ladakh region as a whole which the State government may constitute in consultation with the councils of Leh and Kargil.

Under the law, the government can appoint different dates for the constitution of the district council. In pursuance of this, it is proposed to constitute the council for Leh district in the first place. The district council is to comprise 30 members of whom 26 shall be elected. The remaining members are to be nominated by the Governor from the principal religions minorities and women in the district.

"The council will have executive powers in the district in relation to allotment, use and occupation of and, formulation of development scheme for the district, periodical review of progress of development schemes, formulation and finalisation of budgets, plan as well as non-plan, laying down guideliness for implementation of shcemes at grass- roots level. The council shall also have the powers to collect taxes under the law within the district.

"The members of the council shall elect a chairman, who will also be the chief Executive Councillor of a five-member executive council and shall be responsible for conduct of the business. The four other Executive Councillors shall be nominated by the Chief Executive Councillor."[222]

Here follows the reasons for Enactment for the establishment of Autonomous Development Councils and Inter-District Advisory Council in the Ladakh Region of Jammu and Kashmir.[223]

REASONS FOR ENACTMENT

1. Ladakh region is geographically isolated with a sparse population, a vast area and inhospitable terrain which remains landlocked for nearly six months in a year. Consequently, the people of the area have had a distinct regional identify and special problems distinct from those of the other areas of the State of Jammu and Kashmir. The people of Ladakh have, for a long time, been demanding effective local institutional arrangements which can help to promote and accelerate the pace of development and equitable all-round growth and development having regard to its peculiar geoclimatic and locational conditions, and stimulate fullest participation of the local community in the decision making process.
2. It is felt that decentralisation of powers by formation of Hill Councils for the Ladakh region would give a boost to the developmental activities in Ladakh and meet the aspirations of the people of the said region. The present measure is enacted to

achieve the above object.

3. In view of the urgency of the matter, it is not practicable to consult the consultative committee of Parliament and J & K Legislation. This measure is accordingly being enacted without reference to the said consultative committee.

K. PADMANA BHALLAH
Secretary to the Government of India, Department of Jammu and Kashmir Affirs.

Thereafter, according to the guideliness of Ladakh Autonomous Hill council draft, 26 constituencies were formed. And 22 Congress (I) condidates were declared unopposed, thus election was held only in four constituencies– Phyang, Martselang, Saspol and Kyungam. On 3rd of September, 1995 under the supervision of the Governor of J & K Gen. K.V. Krishna Rao swearing ceremony for the first Ladakh Autonomous Hill development Council was held at the Leh Polo ground. This time 30 members of the new council took the oath. 4 members were nominated by the Governor of J&K. After the gap of one year a delegation from Ladakh went to Dharmsala to meet with Dalai Lama. This delegation had the members of Hill council and some Educationists. H.H. Dalai Lama addressed the delegation and said :

In developed countries, they have neglected the good heart. Here our traditional values have to pay the key role. So in school it should be possible to give education on ethics and morality. In Buddhist communities if children are taught short stories about the life of Buddha and some great teachers of India and Tibet, it will be quite useful.

In the last thirty years many monk students have joined the Tibetan institutions set up at various places in India. I think their number is now around one thousand, so there is great potential. I hope that these monk scholars will help the people in the Himalayas to understand Buddhism and Buddhist culture.

Democracy is a good system. If you look at Buddhism and especially Mahayana the teachings are in the democratic spirit."[224]

Thus after taking the blessing from H.H. Dalai Lama, Ladakh Autonomous Hill development council Leh's members started working for the welfare of Ladakhis in Leh district. However, 1996 was good for the Nuns of Ladakh, as Dutch chomo Funding Group ready to give finance to a Nunnery establishment at Timosogang village.[225] Duchen Rin-po-che also visited Ladakh in the same year and preached people of Ladakh about Buddha teachings.

In 1997 Chogon Rin-po-che started Mune-Mune Maha Mune mantra chanting. One lakh in number at the Tasi-Gya Tsel monastery, Choglamsar. Later he continued this tradition in 1998 and 1999 respectively. On June 1998 H.H. Dalai Lama visited Ladakh and preached people of Ladakh on 37 types of Boddhisattvas practice. On May 1999 he once again visited Ladakh and this time preached on "Dhayan Bhavana of Bodhisattava". During May to June '99 Duchen Rin-po-che visited Chang-Thang, Shachukul, Skrubuchan and Leh, supervised the Amitabha and Mane mantras. Sakya Takchen and Ce Tuk Rin-po-ches also visited Ladakh. They preached and arranged Tantrik rituals at Matho and New monastery of Nyi-ma pa sect at Choglamsar.

Besides, Ladakh Autonomous Hill Development Council, Leh has been keeping its attention for the preservation and protection of Buddhist culture Heritage in Ladakh. During the course of last four years many Mane Tung chur were constructed and Mane walls were renovated. here follows the details :

1.	Mane Tung Chur	Near Petrol Pump	1995
2.	— do —	Near old Bus stand, Leh	1995
3.	— do —	Near SOS, Choglamsar	1995
4.	— do —	near Choglamsar bridge	1996
5.	— do —	Sachukul	1996
6.	— do —	New Bus stand	1996
7.	— do —	In Housing colony	1996
8.	— do —	Near Polo ground	1997
9.	— do —	Near Tukcha	1998
10.	— do —	Above New Bus stand, Leh	1999
11.	— do —	Near I.T.B.F.	1999
12.	Mane wall (Renovated)	Near Moti market	199
13.	Mane wall (Renovated)	Near the New Bus stand	1999
14.	Mane wall (Renovated)	Below the Housing colony	1999
15.	Mane wall (Renovated)	Near the old Bus stand	1998

Today Ladakh has almost all sect of Buddhist monasteries. Here follows the details.

Name of the monastery (1)	Red/Yellow Sect (2)	Buddhist order (3)
Phyang	Red	Drigung pa (or 'Bri-guṅ-pa)
Hemis	Red	Drug pa (or 'Brug-pa)
Spituk	Yellow	Gelug pa
Thikse	Yellow	Gelug pa (or dGe-lugs-pa)
Takna	Red	Drug pa
Tag-Tok	Red	Nyi-ma-pa (or Nying-ma-pa)
Matho	Red	Sakya pa
Shyang	Red	Drigung pa
Shechunkal	Red	Drigung pa
Lamayuru	Red	Drigung pa
Shankar	Yellow	Gelug pa
Stok	Yellow	Gelug pa
Shey	Red	Drug pa
Mahe	Red	Drug pa
Chumatang	Red	Drug pa
Chushul	Red	Drigung pa
Nyoma	Red	Drug pa
Diskit	Yellow	Gelug pa
Hunder	Yellow	Gelug pa
Samstangling	Yellow	Gelug pa
Intsa	Yellow	Gelug pa
Skamphuk	Red	Drug pa
Mulbek	Red	Drug pa
Basgo	Red	Drug pa
Nimo	Yellow	Gelug pa
Likîr	Yellow	Gelug pa
Alchi	Yellow	Gelug pa
Saspol	Red	Drigung pa
Khalatse	Red	Drigung pa
Atiche	Red	Drigung pa
Skrubuchan	Red	Drigung pa
Da	Red	Drigung pa

Hanu	Red	Drigung pa (or 'Bri-guṅ-pa)
Dumkhar	Red	Drug pa (or 'Brug-pa)
Budkharbu	Red	Drigung pa
Rangdum	Yellow	Gelug pa
Sani	Red	Drug pa
Karsha	Yellow	Gelug pa (or dGe-lugs-pa)
Stongde	Yellow	Gelug pa
Zangla		
Bardan	Red	Drug pa
Phugthal	Yellow	Gelug pa
Chemre	Red	Drug pa
Wanla	Red	Drug pa
Mune	Yellow	Gelug pa

In conclusion, Buddhism in Ladakh introduced during 3rd Century B.C. Lo-cha-va Rin-chen-bzang po strengthened it, latter Ladakhi Kings patronaged different sects of Buddhism in Ladakh. After Dogra war Buddhism activities got stagnated, when India got independance, Ladakh automatically came under the admistrative control of Indian Government. Immidiately after the Indo-Pak war Ladakh's religious activities suffered a lot and could not continue till the end of 1999 because duirng this period Ladakh was effected by four wars against China and Pakistan respectively e.g. 1962 Indo-China, 1965 Indo-Pak, 1971 Indo-Pak and in 1999 Indo-Pak proxy wars. However, time and again H.H. Dalai Lama, Tag-can, Che-chang, Cho-gon, Ce-Tuk, Duchen Rin-po-ches visited Ladakh and preached Ladakhis about Buddhist religion, culture and the teachings of Boddhist Acharyas, Bodhsattvas and Lord Buddha. Today, Ladakh Autonomous Hill Development Council, Leh is doing a remarkable job in the preservation and development of Buddhist culture in this region. On 5th November 1999 Ladakh Buddhist Association declared complete Ladakh Bandh. According to the local sources it has been noticed that from 1989 to November 1999 some Buddhist girls married with Muslim boys. So to keep the Buddhist identity LBA thought to fight for union Territory. Later L.B.A. also called Ladakh Bandh on 15th November 1999 and March, 2000 for declaring Ladakh as Union Territory. The L.B.A. authorities argue that in olden days Buddhists were dominant throughout in Ladakh region, now they are limited to only Leh district and Zangskar Tehsil of Kargil district. Therefore for the safeguard of Buddhist population, Government of India should declare Ladakh as Union Territory in which Leh district and Buddhist dominated areas of kargil district included.

NOTES AND REFERENES

1. Kullu = Kulu. It is situated in Himachal Pradesh.
2. Manali : It is a hill station situated in Himachal Pradesh.
3. Zangskar = Zanskar = Zaskar : Until nineteen century Zangskar was attached the Kashmir district of Udampur. Now it is under the administration control of Kargil district of Ladakh. Zangskar is a Tehsil of Kargil district and Padum is its Tehsil headquarter. It is the only Tehsil in Kargil district where about 80 per cent of the Tehsil population belongs to Buddhists.

   "Zangskar includes all the areas along the two main branches of the Zangskar river, in a general direction from south-east of it to north-west. It is bounded by Leh district on the north, by the Rupshu on the east, by Lahul on the south, and by the Kargil and Suru on the west. The southern boundary is formed by the great Himalaya itself, the western by the transversed range of Singa-la, and the northern boundary by the trans-Himalayan Chain. Its greatest length is 72 miles, and mean elevation, as depicted from seven different observation along the Valley, 13,154 feet. The name Zangskar means white copper or brass. Till the end of nineteen century though Zangskar was not under the control of Ladakh Governorship, yet it was closely united to the rest of Ladakh. The physical character – people, race, speech and religion are closely related with the land and people of Leh district. The climate is severe. The spring, summer, and autumn together last little more than five months, after which snowfalls, and at once winter close in, confirming the people and the cattle within doors for half the year. A much greater depth of snow falls here than in Central Ladakh. In the spring it causes avalancehs to such an extent that in the Nunak Valley the people cannot, till a month has passed, get about from village to village for fear of them. Trees are extremely rare; the continuance of snow and the force of the wind are much against their growth. A few population are grown in parts of the district timber. The population was very scanty about 2,500 in 1871, now it is near nine thousand. In 1860, there were about forty three villages in Zangskar containing five hundred houses. Then the tax paid to the Maharaja's Govt. by the Zangskaris was around Rs. 3000/= per year. It was reduced to Rs. 2,000/= in 1869. The Rupshu people brought salt to Zangskar and exchanged it with barley. Some of the salt was taken to Padar and Pangi by a difficult route and there exchanged for rice, butter, skins etc. Part of the salt from Rupshu was also taken on by the Zangskaris to Suru, and exchanged for woollen cloths, barley, a little cash. A fourth line of traffic was with Lahul, whence traders came with cash and buy ponies, sheep and goats. It was only by this branch of trade that enough was introduced into

Zangskar to pay the Govt. tax. Verhere gives the following geological description of this region.

"In Zangskar we find a great mass of genesis and Schist which appears to be the eastern extension of similar rocks which begin in Suru, and after entering largely in the formation of the mountains of he highland of Zangskar area prologed eastward to Rupshu. The genesis, schist, state, and conformable together, and they all dip towards the south and south-west. The limestone appears to be the continuation of a bed of limestone seen in Suru, reposing on the geneiss and schist of the foot of the Ser and Mer peaks." (Cf. Gazatter of Kashmir and Ladak; Vivek Pub., Delhi; P.865).

4. According to Francke, "'aBrog-pa (Dard) is never used here at Nyoma, nor in Rubshu, to signify the pre-Tibetan inhabitants of the country, I believe that the word Mon, which is here always used for them, ------ for on Sven Hedin's new map I find a district near Ruthog called Monyal, a name which evidently refers to a former colonization by Mons or Dards."; (Cf. Francke, A.H. : 'Antiquities of Indian Tibet', S. Chand & Co., New Delhi; PP. 60-61). During investigation in Ladakh, When he camped near Raldrong, he found ruins of a Mon village. Similarly at Nyoma, he was told that there was another deserted Mon settlement above Nyoma on the left bank of the Indus. After crossing Thag-lang pass (17,500 feet high) he reached rGya and found the ancient remains of the village of Ram-rtse which is asserted to have been a Mon settlement; (Cf. Francke, A.H.; Op. Cit. PP. 56-62)

5. Dras = Drass = Drās (or Hembaps) : Lat. 34°26' Long. 75°49' : It is the most westerly portion of the Purik (now Kargil) district and lies along the Valley of the Dras river. More snow falls here than in any other part of Kargil. This is owing "to the great depression in the Himalaya, at the head of the Drās river, which allows the constantly humid vapours of Kashmir to pass to the north of the mountains, where they become condensed by the cold, and are precipitated in rain or snow, according to the season of the year. "In oldern days it was under Purik district which was extended from the Zoji La to Chanagund, near Kargil. A telegraph clerk was then deputed on duty to give information about the Zoji-La. The inhabitants are Shia Musalmans professionally but in physiogromy resemble, the Tartars, with whom they consort freely. Moorcroft says they are great thieves. The crops cultivated are barley, wheat, and buckwheat; the first ripening in about three months, the second in five or six, and the last in about two months. The cattle are ponies, cows, the hybrid between yak and cow, sheep and goats. The farmer, though small, are hardy, active, and tolerably well shaped. The neat cattle are small and generally black. The cattle of Drās are in much better condition than those in any other part of Ladakh, owing to the abundant supply of 'prangos' in summer and its hay in winter. The houses are built of pebbles, cemented with earth,

with terraced roofs." In olden days traders passed through Drās. Here follows the details :

(i) The Srinagar-Leh-Skardu roads after crossing the Zoji-La run down the Drās Valley.

(ii) From Suru to Drās by Umbala. Horses could go for six months.

(iii) From Tilai (Gujrid) to Drās Birok La. Horses could go in September, but in summer the steams formed a serious obstacle.

(iv) A road leads to skardu via the Marpo La, the Shingo river, and the Deosai plains. Horses, it is said, can go for several months in summer, but the road is bad. Cf. Gazetter of Kashmir and Ladakh; Vivek Pub., 1974, PP.301-2

6. Khalatse = Kha-la-che = Kha-la-rtse = Khalsi = Kulsi = Kulluch = Kulatze Lat, 34°19' Long. 76° 57' Elev. 10,130 feet. It is a village of about one hundred twenty eight houses on the bank of Indus river, about 50 miles below Leh. It is a halting place on the road from Srinagar to Leh. During oldern days Srinagar road crosses the Indus by a good wooden bridge a mile or more below the village, today, there is an iron bridge. The river here flows impetuously between steep rocks, the channel bring only 50 feet wide below and 60 feet above. In the first week of August 1999 Khalatse received heavy rainfall, as a result many old big plants of popular and walnut fallen into the gutter and caused heavy losses.

"The old bridge at Khalatse was built by the Dogra invaders, and is 77 feet long and 8 feet broad, with a short railing on each side. High above water during October month was 45 feet. Today it is in ruined condition."

"In olden days there was a small fort built on the northern side of the above bridge. The fort was built by Diwan Hira Singh the first Governor of Ladak = (Ladakh) appointed by tne Maharaja of Jammu and Kashmir State. The garrison then in the fort consisted of nine men. The Khalatse village is on a plateau 250 feet above the river. There is a long strip of cultivated land watered from a side stream. Crops and fruit trees grow on it well, and even laxuriantly, and walnuts and apricots." (Cf: Gazetter of Kashmir and Ladak; Op. Cit.; P. 486)

7. Darel : In oldern days Ladakh was known Darel. This name was derived from Dards, who in those days had colonies throughout in Ladakh. Some scholars belief that Dards were an Indo-Aryan stock and known to Ptolemy as Dardrai who supposed to have sought refuge, much earlier than the kushana; (Cf. Upasak, C.S : 'Early Buddhism in Ladakh'; In : 'Ladakh-Prabha (4)'; P. xix, Leh (1986) & Cunnigham, A. : 'Ancient Georaphy of India', P. 70. Chinese travellers (i.e. Fa-Hsien and Hiuen-tsi'ang) also used Darel country for Ladakh.

8. Francke, A.H.; Op.Cit., P.74.
9. sLes = Leh : The district headquarter of Leh district.
10. rNam-rgyal-rtse-mo : Namgyal-tsemo : ruins on the top of the Leh hill
11. 'aBrog-pai-mkhar : Brog-pai-khar : Dard Castle. The Namgyal-tsemo was called as 'aBrog-pai-mkar in older days.
12. Francke, A.H.; Op.Cit. P.68
13. Ibid.; PP.71-72
14. 'aBrog-pa = Brog-pa : Dard
15. Nyoma : It is a block under Leh district of 28 inhabitted villages.
16. Rubshu (a Rupshu or Ruckohu) : It is the south-eastern district of Ladakh, and one of the loftiest inhabited regions in the world. It is bounded on the north by Ladakh proper, on the east by the Tibetan (Now occupied by China) districts of chum-urti and Rudok, on the south by Lahul & Spiti, and the Tibetan district (Under China) of Tso Tso, and on the west by Zangskar. Its length from Tagalang pass to the head of the Hanle' river is 90 miles, and its mean breadth about 62 miles, which give an area of 5,500 square miles. The valleys have a mean elevation of 15,000 feet. The climate is necessarily severe, and at the same time very dry. In summer the sun at mid-day is very powerful, but in the afternoon a biting wind generally spring up.

    The snow limit is about 20,000 feet. Mountains above this height originate glaciers. The surface of hills is chiefly disintegrated rock, and that of the valley earth or gravel. Vegetation is extremely scant, the only herbage for the flocks beings found by the streams and a little on the hill-sides. There are a few houses and a monastery at karzok, where also there is a little cultivation, the crop of which is often doubt.Cf. Gazetteer of Kashmir and Ladak; Op.Cit., P. 708
17. Da (or Dāh) : Lat. 34° 37' Long. 76° 33' Elev. 9,690'. It is a village in Ladakh on the frontiers of Leh district, on the right bank of the Indus, below Hanu-Yogma. There is a sort of fort here which was built to protect the inhabitants from the Balti raiders. There is also a colony of Buddhist Dards. Cf. Gazetteer of Kashmir and Ladak; Op.Cit., P.281.
18. Rong-chu-rgyud : It is pasture field near Nyoma.
19. Francke, A.H.; Op.Cit. PP. 60-61.
20. During investigation tour I found Ibex carvings on boulders in bulk around Alchi, Khalatse bridges and at the banks of Indus river from Khalatse towards Da, Hanu, and even up to Chobar-la near Pakistan border. Besides human dance carvings can be seen along the motorable road from Khaltse to Tia, Timasgam and its adjoing areas. I have seen Ibex carvings near Taru and villages close to Lower Ladakh. But surprisingly such carving I did not find near Leh and Nyoma where Francke claimed Dard settlements.
21. Francke, A.H : 'Antiquities of Indian Tibet,' Op.Cit., PP.71-72.
22. Arhat : During Buddha period sixteen Arhats were being asked to dissemi-

nate Buddhism. They are : Rahula, Cudapanthaka, Pindolabharadvaja, Panthaka, Nagasena, Gopaka, Abheda, Angaja, Ajita, Vanavasin, Kalika, Vajriputra, Bhadra, Kanakavatsa, Kanakabharadvaja and Bakula Cf. Jack, Firegan : 'Tibet : A Dreamt of image', 1986; P. 132

23. Naga (= Nagas) : Nagas lived in lakes and sea. Nāgārjuna got Prajñāpāramit'a sūtra from a Naga, who led him into the sea and opened up for him the treasury of the Seven Jewels. Cf. Chimpa Lama (Tr.) Taranātha's History of Buddhism in India, Calcutta, 1980; P. 384.

24. Upasak, C.S. : 'Early Buddhism in Ladakh'; In : 'Ladakh-Prabha', Kendriya Buddha Vidya Sansthan, Leh-Ladakh; 1986, P. xvii.

25. Nawang Tsering : 'Buddhism in Ladakh', Sterling Pub. New Delhi., 1979, P. 7 & quoted from *Mahāvaṃsa* (ed. by N.K. Bhagawat, Bombay, 1959) XII. 3; *Dīpavaṃsa* (ed. by B.C. Law, Maharagam, 1959), VIII.4.

26. Maggliputra Tissa : He was the Councellor of As'oka.

27. Majjhātika : He belonged to Varānasi : According to inscription in Bhilsa Topes : Majjhāntika made propagation mission of Buddhism in Kashmir and its adjoing areas. during 3rd Century B.C. Cunningham discovered such inscription in the Tope No.2 of Sanchi group; (Cf. Khosla, Sarla : 'History of Buddhism in Kashmir', Sagar Pub. New Delhi; 1972., P. 14 & quoted from Cunningham, 'Bhilsa Topes,' PP. 287 & 316; Rhys Davis, 'Buddhist India', P. 196; Wilhem Geiger, 'Mahāvams'a', Intro. P. xix says that these were the funeral Urns of Majjh'antika who converted Kashmir to Buddhism and is related in '*Dipvaṃsa*' and '*Mahāvaṃsa*'.

In Ladakh there are some legends under which we can say that Majjhāntika visited many places in Ladakh, for example, according to the inhabitants of Yuru (or Lamayuru) he visited Lamayuru on way to the propogation of Buddhism in Kashmir as well in Ladakh. When he flew towards Ladakh from Kashmir, he first came at Lamayuru. In those days at Lamayuru, there was a big lake and Nagas lived in it. Majjhāntika therefore first sat nearby mountain of lake, then dipped into the lake and through spiritual power emptied the water of lake. Later he forecasted that in future a Buddhist monastery would be established here, latter it help in the propogation of Buddhism in Lower Ladakh.

Some Ladakhi scholars belief that majjhāntika visited Saspol village near Khalatse and predicted that in future Buddhism would have its strong hold in Ladakh, a monastery would also be established in Saspol village.

In September 1994 when I visited Nubra Valley, I was informed that Majjhātika came at Intsa monastery, one can see the imprint on the wall of its one Lha-khang.

Thus, viewing to the above facts we may say that during 3rd Century B.C. Majjh'antika endearvoured his best to propogate Buddhism in Ladakh through his spiritual power, he defeated Nagas who were then in Ladakh.

28. Sumda : It is a village in Leh district near Chilling. When Rin-chen Zang-po came in Ladakh he built one monastery at Sumda.

29. Tiri : It is a village under Nyoma block in Leh district, situated near Kere village and, has about 50 Buddhist houses.

30. Suru Valley : It has a fascinating landscape. Its glaciated topography, with steep gorges, cataracts, alluvial fans, river, terraces and socio-cultural milieu have large potential for the explorers, trekkers, leisure-seekers and acade micians.

    The glacier beds of Nun-Kun caused the formation of the Suru river. At Penze river water gets separated from the catchment of Zangskar, by moving westward, where it is joined by the Shafat-Nallah on its left-bank near the pastures of Gulmatango. Thus the total sprawl on the Suru Valley is about 2900 km. Cf. Prem Singh Jina, 'Ladakh : The Land & the people', Indus Pub. Co., New Delhi; 1996, P. 16

31. Nawang Tsering shakspo: 'An insight into Ladakh', 1993; P. 9 & quoted from Tashi Rabgias, 'Maryul-la dwags kyi snon rabs kun gsal me lon', 1984. However, I didn't find any remains of As'oka paeriod.

32. The fourth legendary Buddhist Council : According to Lama Taranath in the fourth legendary Buddhist council, also known Kanishka's council – 500 Arhats, 500 Bodhisattvas and 500 ordinary Pandits or else 500 Arhats and 500 Mahābhadantas or again of Vasumitra and 400 Bhadantas were present. After the council Bodhisattvas were given more importance then Arhats. The doctrine of Bodhisattva adopted easy methods of charity, ten actions and five prohibitions to attain the desired goal of re-birth in heaven. These ideas were incorporated and further developed in Māhāyana literature; (Cf. Khosla, Sarla; Op.Cit., P.39). The details of Five Prohibitions and ten Five Prohibitions :

    (i) Kill not any living being
    (ii) Steel not
    (iii) Commit not adultery
    (iv) Lie not
    (v) Drink not strong drink; (cf. Khosla, Sarla & quoted from M. Williams, Buddhism, P. 126).

    Ten Prohibitions vide Mahā - Vagga, I.56 are : Abstain from

    (i) Destroying life (Pāṇātipate-prāṇātipāta);
    (ii) taking any thing not given (edinnādāna)
    (iii) Unchastity (abrahmacariyā);
    (iv) Speaking falsely (musā-vāda-mrishā-v'ada);
    (v) Drinking strong drink (Surā)
    (vi) Eating at forbidden times (Vikāla-bhojana)
    (vii) Dancing, singing, music and worldly scenes (visūka);

(viii) Use of high or broad bed;

(ix) Receiving gold or silver

The prohibition of receiving gold or silver or money even for return of teaching was held most important and was obeyed for along time though in the end monasteries became owners of large property and landed estates (Cf. Khosla, Sarla & quoted from M.Williams; Op.Cit., PP.78-79). Emperor Kaniṣha convened the above Buddhist council only because of the fact that he wanted to know the authentic school of Buddhism.

33. Jalandhara : Kaniṣka was the king, of Jalandhara. When sudarśana attained arhat-hood and preached the doctrine in Kashmir, King Kaniṣka visited to Kashmir to meet him. After listened the doctrine from ārya Siṃha Sudarśana, worshipped extensively all caitya-s in the north and also lavishly entertained the samojha-s of the four directions. Cf. Chimpa Lama (Tr.) Taranātha's History of Buddhism in India; Calcutta, 1980, P.91.

34. Kaniṣhka : He became Buddhist on account of his association with King Sinha of Kashmir, latter he convenced a Buddhist council in Kashmir; (Cf. Khosla, Sarla, Op. Cit. P.44)

King Kaniṣhka got a large number of monks assembled in the karṇikavana monastery of Kashmir and, according to the Kashmiris, the third council took place in the Kuvana Vihāra, – a monastery of Jalandhara. Most of the scholars accept the latter view. Cf. Chimpa, Lama (Tr.) Tāranātha's History of Buddhism in India; Calcutta, 1980, PP.92-93.

35. Upasak, C.S.; Op. Cit., P. xix.

36. Chorten (Stupa) : Chorten is the combination of two words 'chod' and rTen' means worship or 'a worship place', while constructing the chorten the following things put inside – Religions books, ash of dead body small pieces of precious things, small quantity of foodstuffs, Mantras or religions scripts. Cf. Tsering Sonam (Tr. Prem Singh Jina) an unpublished paper.

37. Drās = Dras = Dras : Cf. Ref. No.5.

38. Francke, A.H. : Op.Cit., P. 94 (Cf. footnote) & Upasak, C.S.; Op.Cit.

39. Upasak, C.S.; Op.cit.

40. Khosla, Sarla; Op.Cit., P.45

41. Acharya Nagarjuna was the founder of Madhyamika theory of Buddhism. He wrote Prajñaparmita which consists 'Mythical discourses attributed to Buddha and addressed mostly to supernatural hearers on vultue peaks'; (Cf. Khosla, Op.Cit., P.161 & Waddell, P. 125).

The traditional account agrees that Nāgārjuna was born as a Brahmin in South India. After entering the Buddhist Order, he is said to have thoroughly studied the Buddhist scriptures then available. But he failed to be satisfied with these and started searching for more texts. Thus he eventually obtained the Prajñāpārmitā sūtras from a Nāga. These texts fully satisfied him and he devoted the rest of his life in the propogation of their teachings. Cf. Lama Chimpa (Tr.): 'Tāranātha's History of Buddhism in India', Op.Cit. P. 384.

42. Khosla, Sarla; P. 68
43. Patliputra : King As'oka, the great-grandson of King Bimbisāra, transferred his capital from Rājagṛha to Pāṭliputra. Latter he invited sixty thousand arhats and honoured them by offering high seats. At the end, he offered to each monk robes worth a lakh. On the same night, the King, along with his attendants started on the shoulders of the most powerful yakṣa for visiting the caityas, in seven days, completed his pilgrimage of the caityas raised all over Jambudvipa in honour of the Jewels. Cf. Lama, Chimpa; Op.Cit. PP.52, 62-63.
44. Khosla; Op.Cit., P.68
45. Darel : Pl. see Ref. No. 7
46. Lesser Vehcile : Hinayana school
47. Lo-han : It means Arhat
48. Tusita : Heaven
49. Upasak, C.S.; Op.Cit.
50. Udyāna : It is the birth place of Guru Padama Sambha.
51. Upasak, C.S.; Op.Cit; PP xx-xxi & referred from Beal, S : 'Records of Buddhist world', PP.133-135; Life of Hieun-tsiang, PP. 66-67, Watters, T: 'On the Trands of Yaun Chwang', P. 240.
52. Upasak; Op. cit.
53. Vihara : Monasteries or Buddhist monasteries which are constructed at least 400 feet away from the village society. In Ladakh these are mostly constructed on the hillocks of the nearby village.
54. Chaityas : These are similar as stupas or chortens (Buddhist monuments).
55. Khosla; Op.cit., PP. 48-49
56. Nawang Tsering : 'Buddhism in Ladakh', Op.Cit. P.8. About Mulbe's huge rock sculpture of Maitreya, Moorcroft made the following note : "Near the end of this day's journey, the road passed between the foot of the mountains on the right of the valley and an insulated pillar of rock, about fifty feet high. On the face of this was sculptured the figure of one of the Tibetan divinities named Chamba. It differed from the same representation in the temples is being decorated with the Brahminical code, hanging from the left shoulder and over the right hip. The figure was naked, except round the waist, and was about twenty-four feet high, but the lower part was concealed by a low wall in front; the upper had been protected by a screen projecting over it from the rock, but this was gone, leaving only the holes in which the pins that had fastened it, had been inserted." However, Francke believed that like śakti temple at Chhatṛārhī

in Chambā state, there is a four-armed Brahmā, carrying a robary and a water-pot, and accompained by a pair of geese, date from about 700 A.D.; the Maitreya of Mulbe would be of the same time; (Cf. Francks, Op.Cit., P. 102).

57. Nawang Tsering : 'Buddhism in Ladakh', Op.Cit. P. 8

58. Khosla; Op.Cit.; P. 54

59. Sron-btsan-gam-po = Sron-tsan-gam-po : He was bron 600/617 A.D. On the crown of his head there was an excrescence believed to be a symbolic representation of Buddha Amitabha. Although it was very bright and full of lustre, yet he used to cover it with a red satin head-hand. At the age of thirteen he ascended the throne. During this period some images were discovered, in certain caverns of rocks and recesses of mountains, many self-created images of chanressig the divine mother Tara Hayagriva and other gods, besides many incriptions including the six mystic syllables: Om-main-padma-hum.

The king visited these images and oblations to them with his own hands. With the help of these subjects he built a lofty nine-storied palace on the top of the hill, where Potala now stands, built out of its ruins. He had immense armies, besides, innumerable reserve troops of spirits over whom, by force of his charms he had great command. The fame of his wisdom and martial valour of this double-headed prince, as he was called from the excrescence over his head, reached the border countries, whose sovereigns sent ambassadors to his court with letters and rich presents. He returned their kindness in a way that was most becoming in a sovereign of his rank. Sron-tsan-gam-po was by the time was young enough evinced great intelligence and sagcity indealing with his dependent princes and imporving friendship with independent potentates. There was no written language in Tibet. Sron-tsan-gam-po was the first king in Tibet who sent Sambhota with sixteen scholars to Kashmir to learn language and discover such script which would serve the written uniform language for Tibet. Thereafter through his direction may texts of Buddhism were translated in Tibetan language from Sanskrit. Later when he married with two princesses — one from Nepal and other from China, he was influenced by Buddhism as both the princesses brought Buddhist images from their respective countries. Thereafter, Sron-tsen-gam-po erected many Buddhist temples in Tibet and also invited various Buddhist scholars from India. Besides he himself received instructions of secret Tantra and got initiations of Arya Avalokitesvara; (Cf. Das, Sarat chandra : 'Early History of Tibet'; In : 'Encyclopaedia of Tibet'; Vol. I.; Sharma, S.K. & Sharma, Usha (ed.); 1996, 71-72.

60. The Nepal princess was the daughter of Jyota Verma King of Nepal, who brought him seven princious dowries, the images of Aksobhiya and Maitreya and a sandal - image of Tara, the gem named Ratnadeva a mendi-

cant's Platter made of lapis-lazuli or Vaidurya; (Cf. Das, Sarat chandra; Op.Cit., P. 73).

61. Sron-btsan-gam-po when heard the report of the extraordinary beauty of the princess Hun-shin-kun-ju, the daughter of Senge-tsanpo of China, he sent his Prime Minister Gar with hundred officers to China. After repeated negotiations the proposal was agreed to. Many stories are recorded in connection with this marriage of which I here give one. As the number of condidates for the princess's hand was very great, the king, unable to decide whom to choose or whom to reject, at last declared that he should bestow the princess on that prince whose minister by dint of sharpness of sense and quickness of understanding would stand first in merit and intelligence. In the first ordeal, the King laid before the assembled ministers a buckler constructed of coil of turquoise, with one and terminating in the centre and the other at the edge. He required them to pass a string through the aperture of the coil from one and to the other. It was minister Gar, who tying one and of a thread to the narrow waist of a queen ant, gently blew if forward through the coil. The ant, dragging the thread easily, came out at the other and to the great wonder of all. The king, not liking to send his favourite daughter to such a distant and barbarous country as Tibet, devised repeated trails in all of which the cunning minister acquitted himself well. The reluctance of the King was at last overcome by various contrivances, and he at last determined to decide the fate of his daughter finally. He ordered 500 smart girls of the princess's age to be dressed in the same kind of apparel as his daughter, and exhibited them before the assembed ambassadors along with the princess herself. The shrewd Tibetan, never wanting in resources, had studied the countenance of the princess; moreover being secretly infromed of the King's design, he had taken some hints about the identification of the princess from an old nurse, in the royal household. By these means, the minister Gar at once recognized the real princess, and gently pulling the edge of here robe, he claimed her for his liege lord. The trials ended here, when it was fully settled that the princess should go to Tibet, she addressed the king, "Sir as it has pleased your Imperial Majesty to send me a Bod, a country where there is no region, I pray that you will allow me to take with me the great image of Buddha, and several volumes of Buddhist scriptures, besides a few treatises on medicine and astrology." The king accordingly granted her prayer and gave them a parts of her dowry. Hearing that Tibet was a very poor country, he sent with the princess heaps of gold and silver for her use in Tibet; (Cf. Das, Sarat Chandra; Op.Cit., P. 73).

62. Puri, B.N. : 'Buddhism in Central Asia; Motilal Banarsidas Pub., Delhi; 1987; P. 149 (Cf. foot note).

63. Sambhota : He was the son of Anu and being sent to Kashmir with companions, to study carefully the Sanskrit language and thereby obtain

access to the sacred literature of the Indian Buddhists. The King of Tibet also instructed Sambhota and to devise means for the invention of a written language for Tibet, by adapting the Sanskrit alphabet to the phonetic peculiarities of the Tibetan dialect. King furnished the members of the mission with a large quantity of gold to make presents to their Indian professors. Sambhota along with his companions safely reached their destination in Aryavarta, where, under the Buddhist sage Livikara, they acquired a thorough knowledge of Sanskrit and of sixty-four different characters known in the Arya land. Under Pandit Devavid Sinha they learnt the Kalapa, Chandra and Sarasvata grammers of the Sanskrit language. They also mastered the twenty-one tretises of aphorisms and mystricism of the Buddhist creed. After returning to Tibet, they propitiated Manjusri, the god of learning, and framed the system of Tibetan characters, viz., the U-chan or "letters provided with heads" (mantra-s) adopted from the Devanagari, and the U-me or "headless" from the wartu, and thus introduced a copious system of written language into Tibet. They composed the great grammatical work called sum chu dag-yig; (Cf. Das, Sart chandra; Op. cit., P. 72)

64. Das, Sarat Chandra; Op.cit.; PP.72-73.

65. Chenressig = Avalokitesvara is the hidden beyong wherein creatures of dust and of spirit become the vision of light. In Him the entire oeuvre of devotion becomes a journey of beauty and purity, of truth and discernment, of smile and harmony, in a world of passing dreams, passing time, underlying the enternal dynamics of creativity and beauty, of self-development and transcendance. These infinite possibilities of creativity flow into hymns and miniatures, sculptures and paintings, ever evolving into the multiplicity of forms of Avalokita. In the process Avalokita assimilates the manifestations of Lokeśvaras an integeation of many levels of ideas and deeps of thoughts. The new seeks stability in the experience of lived memories. Popular iconic vocabulary becomes the essence of ever-renewing theogony. From an attendant acolyte of Amitābha in Sukhāvatī-vyūha, Avalokita gained independence as a separate deity in his own right, while the worship of his prototype Brahmā ceased,until the great 'Adi-Śaṅkarā-cārya resurrected Brahmā the abstract Brahman. The Potala Lokeśvara holds the mysteries of Harihara, the devarāja cult and a key to the enigmatic faces at Angkar. Entire systems of the thought lie embedded in the silent enigmas of Avalokitasvara Lokeśvara. Cf. Lokesh Chandra, 'The thousand-armed Avalokitesvara', IGNCA, New Delhi; P.9.

66. Pandit Kusara : He was a Buddhist scholar belongs to India.

67. Pandit Sankara Brahmana : He was a Buddhist scholar belongs to India.

68. Pandit Sila Maju : He was a Buddhsit scholar belongs to Nepal.

69. Hwa-shan-Maha-tshe : He was a Buddhist scholar belongs to China.

70. Das, Sarat chandra; Op.cit., P.74

71. Thi-sron-tsan (= Ti-song-Detsan in the = Trisong Detsen); According to the chronologist Buton, he was in the Kunju's womb, his mother saw in a vision that a saintly prince would be born of her. She, therefore, kept aloof from unholy things. The old queen Nam-nan, jealous of queen Kunju. When the Kunju delivery time came, Nam-nan induced one of her mid-wives to give her a kind of anaesthetic liquor, through which Kanju became insensible and soon gave birth to a son, which the wicked Nam-nan, by bribing replaced it by a female child. As soon as Kunju recovered her sense, she was surprised to see a daughter instead of a son. Soon after, King got the report that queen Nam-nan gave birth to a son. Queen Kunju then strongly suspected her jealous partner, but in the absence of witnesses, being unabled to change Nam-nan with any foul motive, kept her sorrows to herself. Later King arranged a grand festive. All the nobles, chiefs and ministers of the realm assembled at the palace, the King seated the prince and princess on either side and taking a cupful of wine in his hand, address the former : "My son, take this gold cup of wine and with your tender hand offer it to your maternal uncle." To the utter amazement of all present, the prince at once presented it to the Chinese prince whom he thus address : 'I Thi-srong-de-tsan am thy nephew. Nam-nan is not my mother, though she has nursed me for a period of three years. I now meet my uncle, and my heart rejoices to behold him." These words of the infant prince struck all the courtiers and ministers with wonder. Nam-nan's wickedness was now at last revealed, and she was overwhelmed with shame. Kunju was transported with joy when the King presented the child to her; therefore, when Thi-sron-de-tson came into the throne he was only thirteen years old. And his ministers were divided into two factions, designated the "Buddhist" and the "Heretic". The first faction advised the young King to encourage Buddhism, while their antagonists exhorted him to extirpote Buddhism from Tibet, which according to them had been productive of pernicious consequences. In spite of the opposition, the King, having a great inclination for Buddhism, sided with the former; (Cf. Das, Sarat, Chandra; Op.cit., P.76).

72. Santaraksita : He was the foremost scholar of his time and master of all aspects of the Mahāyāna teachings, supported the Sangha in both India and Tibet by transmitting his lineages and knowledge to hundreds of disciples. He was born to a royal family in Sahora in the small village of Sabhar during the reign of Gopāla, the first king of the Pāla dynasty. Ordained by Jñānagarbha, the Svātantrika-mādhyamika scholar and writer, he received the Vinaya Lineage of the Buddha's son Rāhula, which had been continued by Nāgārjuna and a lineage of prominent masters. Mastering the teaching of the second and third Turnings, and the works of Nāgārjuna, Maitreya, Asaṅga, Dharmakīrti, and their commentators, he held the lineages of all Mahāyāna phiiosophical traditions and forged the system known as Yogācāra-Svātantrika-mādhyamika. He explicated his

views on Mādhyamika philosophy in Madhyama-kāla=mkāra-kārikā and its commentary and again in his commentary on Jñānagarbha's Satyadvayavibhaṅga. Cf. Crystal Mirror, Vol. VI, Dharma Pub., 1971, P.370.

73. Padma-Sambhava : Padmasambhava, embodiment of Dharmakāya, Sambhogakāya, and Nirmāṇakaya of the Tathāgatas and Vidyādhara of all forms of enlightened knowledge, transmitted the Inner teachings of the Mantrayāna to Tibet. Although he probably lived at bSam-yas for only a short time, most gter-ma texts agree that he manifested in Tibet for about 111 years, guiding his diciples practices at retreat centres in remote sacred places. While at bSam-yas, he subjugated all human and non-human obstacles to Dharma transmission, and blessed the land of Tibet; he also transmitted the Inner teachings to Khri-srong lde-bstan and other major disciples, establishing the basis of the bKa'-ma and gter-ma transmission continued by succeeding generations of rNying-ma masters to the present day. Cf. Crystal Mirror, Vol. VI., P.268.

74. Udyana : Cf. Ref. No. 50.

75. Chorten : Cf. Ref. No. 36.

76. Samye = bSamyes : It was founded by Santarakshta and Padmasambhava under King Trhisong Detsen (reigned 755-795) was the oldest Buddhist monastery in Tibet and the first in which Tibetans themselves were trained as monks. Although now destroyed, it is described by Buston, Lama Tsenpo, and kyentse, and is pictured in a Tibetan thanka ascribed to the sixteen-seventeenth century in the Albert L. Shelton Collection in the New York Museum. The location of the monastery is 50 km/35 miles southest of Lhasa and about 5 km/3 miles north of the Yarlung Tsangpo river. Cf. Finegan, Jack; Op.cit., P. 140.

77. Hwashan Mahayana : After arriving in Tibet Hwashan Mahayana endeavoured to explain their theory of religion and up to some extend he was able to convinced Tibetans. Therefore, he made confusion by interpreting in a strange way the theories of Buddhism, converted the ignorant classes of men to his tenets. King Thi-Sron-de-tsan found great doubts as to the correctness of Hwashan's theories. Then he invited Pandit Kamalasila from India to expose his fallacies. Kamalasila held long controversies with Hwashan and in the end defeated him.

78. Kamalsila : He was the disciple of Santarakṣita, master of philosophy and Sialectic, continued Sāntarakṣita's work in his teaching, writing and other activities on behalf of the Dharma in both India and in Tibet. His work in Tibet was foreseen by his master Śāntarakṣita, who told Khri-srong lde-btsan that the Dharma in Tibet would not be troubled by spread of heretical doctrines. Sāntaraksita predicted however, that two distinct schools would arise based on differing interpretations of the doctrine and the manner of attaining enlightenment, the great paṇḍita advised the King to

call upon his disciple Kamalaśīla when controversies arose, Kamalaśīla, to whom the master had transmitted all his knowledge, would uphold Ś'antarakṣita's teachings and put an end to controversy. Cf. Crystal Mirror, Vol. VI; P.374.

79. Das, Sarat Chandra; Op.cit., P.77.
80. Muni-tsanpo : He was Kind hearted person and commenced his independent reign with a generous determination of raising all his subjects to the same level. He ruled that there should be no distinction between poor and rich. He compelled the wealthy to share their riches with the indigent and helpless, and to make them their equal in all the conforts and conditions of life. His mother was not happy with his popularity among people, therefore, gave poison to him, as a matter of fact she was interested to place her youngest son on the throne; (Cf. Das, Sarat chandra; Op.Cit., P.77).
81. Das, Sarat Chandra, Op.cit., P.77
82. Mutig-tsanpo : He was the youngest son of Thi-sron-de-tsen and at the age of eight years received the crown.
83. Ralpachen : He was born between 846 and 860 A.D. He favoured Buddhism and built a new nine-storeyed temple, of which the three middle of brick, and the topmost three of wood. In the upper floors he kept Buddhist scriptures, images, and model chorten. In the middle floors he accommodated the Pandits and translators of the holdy writs, and the ground floors he received for the use of his court and state affairs. He introduced standard weights and measures similar to these used in China, and thereby preserved fraudulent practices regulation of India for the discipline and guidance of the clargy, and commanded his lay people to follow the statutes as promulgated by his illustrious predecessors. During the reign of this great monarch, there arose a dispute between Tibet and China. Ralpachen sent a powerful army to invade China. Province after province of the celestial empire fell before his victorious arms and annexed to Tibet. Later Hwashan and Lopan interceded to put a stop to further bloodshed between that the monarchs. After the agreement at Gungu-Meru the boundary was fixed between two countries. He was a good administrator, punished the wicked and rewarded the good. At the age of forty eight, Landarma prepared foul act and with the assistance of two ruffians killed him; (Cf. Das, Sarat Chandra, Op.cit.; PP.78-79).
84. Das, Sarat Chandra; Op.cit.; PP. 78-79
85. Nying-ma : The lineage of this order is described as beginning with the Adi Buddha, who is known by various names as Samantabhadra (Tibetan Kuntur bzang po, pron. Kuntu sangpo) Vajradhara (Tibetan rDo-rje 'chang, pron. Dorje chhang), and Vajrasattva (Tibetan rDo-rje sems dpa, pron. Dorje Sampa). The lineage enters the level of human tradition with dGa'rab rdo rje (pron. Garap Dorje), an Indian or Tibetan teacher considered an

emanation of Vajrasattva. Garap Dorje taught his disciple 'Jam dpal bshes gnyen (pron. Jampe, Shenyan), Jampe Shenyen taught Śri-Singha, and Śri-Singha taught Padmasambhava, the most eminentpersonage in the entire lineage, as well as Padmasambhava's contemporaries and associates, the Indian Vimalamitra, the Tibetan Vairocana, and King Trhisong Detsen (reigned 755-797). Finegan, Jack : 'Tibet : A Dreamt of Image', 1986, P. 82.

86. Ge-lam-kesar (or Kesar) : According to Dr. Jina "Kesar is the son of the heavenly god, who sent him down the earth in a human form to help human beings. He even changed his appearance and turned himself into the grab of a beggar when he was looking at the land of princess Breugmo. Her parents rejected him. He then performed many feats of bravery." Cf. Jina, prem Singh, 'Ladakh : The Land & the people', Op.cit. P. 94.

87. Guru-Tsan-gyet : Padma Sambhava is known called by eight names, Garu-Tsan-gyet.

88. Sakti : Lat. 34° 5'

Long. 77° 50'

Elev. 13,500'

It is a large village at head of the chimray valley passed on the Changchenmo route about 4½ miles above Chimray. It is situated at the junction of two streams; up the western one a road leads over the waris pass to the village of Tainyar (Tayar) and thence to Nubra. The road to Zingral camp (3½ miles) leads up the stream which runs down south-west from the changla pass. The Chimray Valley from Sakti the Indus is well cultivated in a succession of teraces. Ascent between Sakti and Zingral very steep, being the best part of the ascent to, the changla pass. Cf. Gazeteer of Kashmir and Ladak; Op.cit. P. 714.

89. Padum (= Padam) : Lat. 32° 28' Long. 76° 56' Elev. 11,873'

It is the Tehsil headquarter of Zangskar Tehsil in Kargil district and situated on the left bank of the Zangskar river, 5 miles above its junction with a tributary from the west, and at the south-east angle of a plain lying between the two rivers. It was formerly the capital of Zangskar. It is still, however, owing to its central position, considered the chief place of the district. Two routes lead from here to Leh, one most used being via Zangla, Yalchang, and Lamayuru. Being surrounded by high mountains, which intercept all moisture, there is very little vegetation, and no trees are to be seen. The plain to the north-west is, however, partially cultivated. The river is crossed, opposite the village, by rather an insecure rope bridge, high above the stream which at the end of June was deep, rapid, and muddy. Cf. Gazeteer of Kashmir and Ladak; Op.cit;. P. 639.

90. Kargil : Lat. 34° 34' Long. 76° 11'. Elev 8,787'.

It is the district headquarters of Kargil district and situated at the junction of Suru and Pashkyum (or wakha) rivers. There is a fort here commenting the road at the junction of the rivers. It stands about 250 yards above the bridge, on the left bank. It is of the usual style, namely, a square with corner bastions. The walls are 25 feet high and loopholed in two tiers. The garrison was having one native officer and fifteen sepoys and was commanded from the collectorate above. The collectorate was at the top of the village, and comprised some neat and commodions buildings. From Kargil the road crosses the river in front of the fort by three or four log bridges, now iron bridgė is used, the road then leads across a high undulating tract of gravel, which occupies the angle between the two rivers, and then descends into the Paskyam Valley. The successive reaches on either shore are occupied by flourishing little hamlets; these are surrounded by their corn-fields and plantations of willow and poplar, and present a pleasing picture of prosperity amidst the bare rocks around. Cf. Gazeteer of Kashmir and Ladak; Op.cit., P. 440

91. Ladakh : Kargil & Zangskar (J & K Tourism Pub.); P. 27.

92. Mahaghyalila Marghat : Maha-Ghyuya-lila-Marghat, famous meditation centre for Māhāyani monks.

93. According to Ladakh chronical Padma. Sambhava not only suppressed the demons in Zangskar, but he was coming/going to Leh (or Kashmir) one Dakini was after him, when Padma Sambhava reached near the present Gurudawara she started throwing stones upon him, but Padma Sambhava hid behind a stone. Later when Dakini hid behind the '*Ralpa-Ri*', Padma-Sambhava got chance to suppress her. However, some Ladakhi historians belief that when Padma-Sambhava reached near Nimo village a demon shot an arrow at him, but after taking refuge behind a rock he safed his life. Latter with his spiritual power he killed the demon. The imprint of his body can been seen at this place; (Cf. Nawang Tsering Shakspo : 'an insight into Ladakh; 1993; P.10 & quoted from Snellgrone, D.C. & skorupski, Tadeusz : 'The Cultural Heritage of Ladakh', Delhi; 1980).

94. Vohra, Rohit : 'Dating of a Maitreya Relief of the Mid-8th Century; from Sumda Chen'; South Asian studies 9, 1993. PP. 97-103.

95. Skyid-lde-nyima-gon (900-930 A.D.) : According to Francke skyid-lde-nyima-gon's period was 975 to 1000 A.D. He was the grandson of Langdarma (or gLang-dar-ma). When elder queen yumstan (or Yum-brten) and her supporters banished him, he came to western Tibet and founded a castle in Purang (or sPu-rangs). In those days Dards were living there. He had great battle with them and at last won the battle. Thereafter Dards praise him as Sun-lord. Here follows the further details :

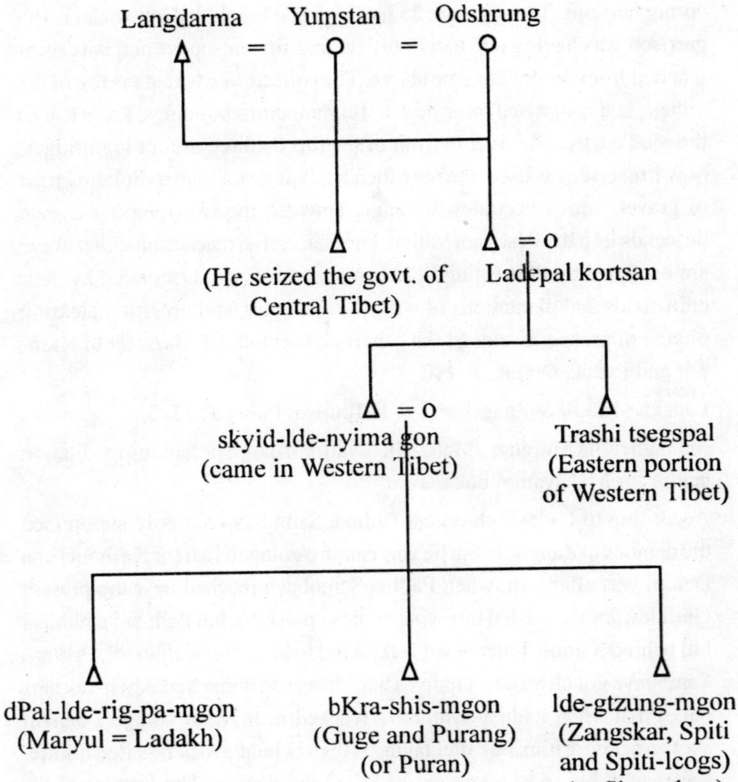

According to Francke bKra-shis-mgon seized Puran; and the youngest lde-gtzung-mgon became King of the province Shan-shun

Source : Das, Sarat Chandra; Op.cit;. PP. 90-91.

96. Sheh (= Shay) : Lat. 34° 5'. Long 77° 45'

It is a village on the right bank of the Indus, passed on the Changechenmo route at 7 miles above Leh. Road heavy for first few miles out of Leh, owing to sandy natural of soil. There is a monastery here, also an old palace of the local Gyalpos (now ruined), and at the monastery has a copper gilt image of Buddha, 30 feet high. Cf. Gazeteer of Kashmir and Ladak; Op.cit., P. 736.

97. Francke, A.H. : 'The Inaguration of the Central Tibetan, dyansty and its

First Kings, About 900-1400 A.D.', In : 'Encyclopaedia of Tibet; Sharma, S.K. & Sharma, Usha (ed.); 1996, P. 109.

98. Cf. Ref. No. 95

99. Ladakh : In olden days it was popularly known Maryul

100. dPal-lde-rig-pa-mgon (Spal-ki-mgon) : He received Ladakh proper, from the Zoji pass to Rutog. His position was not only the largest, but certainly the most beautiful part of the empire; (Cf. Francke, A.H.; Op.cit., PP. 109-110.)

101. Tho-ling (mtho-gling) : It is a famous monastery in western Tibet. Yeshes-'od was the founder of this gompa which played an important role in the propogation of Buddhism in mNga'-ris and in the subsequent second phase of Buddhism developed in this region. Cf. Nawang Tsering; Op.cit. P. 9

102. Lha-lama-yeshes-od : He was formerly known 'Khor-re, latter he became monk and changed his name to Yeshes-od. The following figure shows the details :

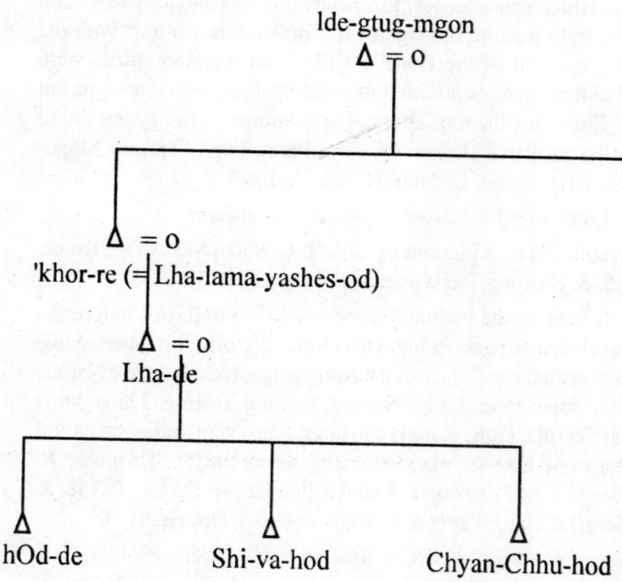

Source : Das, Shart Chandra; Op.cit., P. 91

103. Rin-chen-Zang-po (= Rin-chen-bzang-po or Rin-C'en-bzaṅ-po (1958-1055) : He was the great translator and popularly as the builder of 108 temples and chaples in western Tibet. Cf. Finegan, Jack; op.cit., P.60

104. Nawang Tsering; Op.cit., P. 9

105. Nawang Tsering; Op.cit., P. 9 & Nawang Tsering slakspo Op. cit., PP. 12-13 and Handa, O.C. : 'Role of Rin-chen-bZang-po in the Development of Buddhism', In : Proceed of the the National Seminar on 'Preservation and Development of Himalayan Culture', 1994; PP. 5-7

106. Some historians belief that Rin-chen-Zang-po visited Kashmir in three occasions.

107. Handa, O.C.; Op.cit., P. 12

108. Ibid; P. 8

109. Ibid; P. 8

110. Naropa : He was the famous disciple of Tilopa under the guidance of his guru he attained the heightest realization and received the full transmission of the Mahāmudrā and became great scholar, siddha. Cf. Crystal Mirror, vol. VI., Dharma Pub., U.S.A., 1984, P. 354

111. Lamayuru : It is the sub gonpa of Phyang monastery now has independent administrative control. According to the legendary, there was once a lake at the foot of the cliff inhabited by snake-spirits of the Bon religion, they were driven away by a wandering Buddhist ascetic who offered them grains of rice which marveleously formed themselves into a swastika and turned to the right making the sign of the Buddha, in contrast with the opposite arrangement of the Bon Swastika, and the Bon spirits were complelled to flee, being in addition pursued by three lions that came out of the lake. From this the monastery is also known as the gyung drung dgon pa or the Swastika Gonpa. Cf. Jina, Prem Singh 'Tibetan Manuscripts and Inscriptions of Ladakh' Himalaya, 1998, P. 73

112. Lochawa = Lotsawa = Lo-tsa-wa = Lotsaba : Translator

113. Petech, Luciano : 'The Kingdom of Ladakh C. 950-1842 A.D.'; Roma, 1977, P. 165. & Nawang Tsering Shakspo; Op.cit., P. 13.

114. Zangkhul : It falls on the Padum-kishtwar trakking trail; just before the ascent to the Omasi-la pass begins. This monastery is in fact situated like a swallow's nest cn the rock face of the Ating gorge. Here in a cave Naropa meditated for some time. Latter Siddha Nawang Tsering, Lama Jotpa Dorje, Lama Skarma, Lama Kangla choslegs, Lama stag chang Raspa and Lama Norbu came here for meditation; Cf. Tashi Dorje : '*Zangskar Ki Pramukh Gonpao ka Parichaya*', Ladakh-Prabha (4); Op.cit., P. 148. & Ladakh : Kargil & Zangskar (J & K Tourism Pub.); Op. cit., P. 30.

115. Ladakh : Kargil & Zangskar; J & K Tourism Pub.; Op.cit., P. 30.

116. Byang-chub-'od = Chyan-chhu-hod; Cf. Ref. No. 102.

117. Das, Sarat Chandra; Op.cit., P. 91

118. Ibid., PP. 91-92.

119. Kadampa = bKa-gdam-pa order : The bKa' gdams pa (pron. Kadam-pa) constitute the order "bound by command," and they developed into the gsar ma bKa' gdams pa (pron. Sarma Kadam-pa) or New Kadam-pa, also

known as the dGe lugs pa (pron. Gelug-pa) or order of the "model of virtue" which, in distinction from the "red hat" (zhwa dmar, pron. shamar) orders, is popularly known as the "yellow hat" (zhwa ser, pron. Shaser) order. Jack Finegan; Op. cit., PP. 98-99.

120. Ol-de : Cf. Ref. No. 102.

121. Spituk monastery : dPe-thub-monastery : This monastery is situated 8 Km. far away from Leh along the Leh-Srinagar Highway. It stands prominently on the top of a hillock commanding a panoramic view of the Indus valley for miles. Many icons of Buddha and fine thankas are to be found in this 15th Century gompa. The gompa (or gonpa) also houses a collection of ancient masks, antique arms, and an inspiring image of Mahakal. The face of the Kali image is kept covered and is revealed only at the annual function in January. Cf. Ladakh a publication of J & K Tourism Deptt.

122. Vries, Sjoerd - Jan de : 'Notes on the History and Iconography of Bakula'; In : Recent Research on Ladakh; London, 1983, P. 30

123. Tse-de : He introduced the method of calculating time by the system of cycles of years, called Rab-Jun. During his period many translators viz. Ssan kaar Lochava, Rva Lochava, Nan Lochava, London Serab etc. engaged in translation works of Sanskrit Buddhist texts in Bodhi language. Cf. Das, Sarat Chandra; Op.cit., P. 92.

124. Stongdey monastery : It is 18 kms. to the north of Padum, on the road loading to Zangla in Zangskar Tehsil. It is the second largest monastery in Zangskar inhabited by a resident of about 60 dGe-lugs-pa monks. Cf. Ladakh : Kargil & Zangskar; Op.cit., P. 28.

125. Lha-chen-rgyal-po (= lha-C'en rgyal-po) : He did remarkable job after establishing Likir monastery near Saspol. In olden days Likir was a town on the great trade road, as the road in those days came to Leh by Tingmogang, close to the monastery is said to have been planted by Lha-chen-rgyal-po. Cf. Francke, A.H.; Op.cit., P. 110

126. Likir (= Li-Kyir) : founded in the 11th Century A.D. and rededicated to a different monastic order in the 15th century A.D., its earlier *gompa* was destroyed in a fire. The present *gompa* date back to the 18th Century. Cf. Ladākh, Pub. of Govt. of India, Delhi; 1990; P.11

127. bTsong-kha-pa : Also known as rJe Rin po che or the precious ruler. As his name reflects, Tsongkhapa was born in the district of Tsong kha, meaning Onion Valley, in the vicinity of lake kokonor in Amdo, where in 1578 the kumbum monastery was founded at his birth place. Cf. Finegan, Jask; Op.cit., P. 100

128. Francke; Antiquities of Indian Tibet; Op.cit. P.88

129. Likir (= Klu-dkyil) : Ancient town near Saspol; Op.cit.

130. mchod-rten : chorten or Stūpa.

131. Francke, A.H. : Antiquities of Indian Tibet'; Op. Cit., P. 88
132. Petech, Luciano; Op. cit., P. 77.
133. Francke, A.H. : 'Antiquities of Indian Tibet', Op. Cit., PP. 105-106.
134. Francke, A.H.; In : 'Encyclopaedia of Tibet', Op.cit., P. 110
135. Ibid.
136. Wanla : (= Waṃ-le or Wanla) : Lat. 34° 18' Long. 76° 53' Elev. 10,900'. This village is situated on the left bank of the Wanla stream, lying 6 miles south-east of Lamayuru. It is passed between the letter and Hofata, on the route from Kistwar to Leh (via Zangskar). Cultivation here in July rich and luxuriant. Cf. Gazeteer of Kashmir and Ladak; Op.cit., P. 849.
137. Kha-la-tse; Cf. Ref. No. 6
138. Drigung-pa order (= 'Bri-guṅ-pa order) : It is a sub-sect of the bKa'-brgyud-pa order.

    It was founded by the Phakmotru-pa's pupil 'Jig rten mgon po (pron. Jigten Gompo), (1143-1217). In 1179 'Jig rten mgon po established the 'Bri gung (Drigung) monastery (128 km/80 miles northeast of Lhasa from which the sect took its name. Jigten Gompo was also himself known as 'Bri gung rin po che (Pron. Drigung Rincpoche). Finegan, Jack; Op.cit., P. 96.
139. Petech, Luciano; Op.cit.; PP. 166-67
140. Lhargyal = Lha-rgyal (1250-1275 A.D.) His full name was Lha chen Kunga Namgyal. This name has been preserved to us on an ancient sculpture near the village of Daru. The principal sculpture represents a *Vajrapani* seems to have been the favourite deity of this King. Cf. Francke, A.H.; In : Encyclopedia of Tibet, P. 111
141. Nawang Tsering Shakspo; Op.cit., P. 17
142. gon-pos : Eight manifestations of mgon-po, the nath (guardian deities). Cf. Nawang Tsering Shakspo; Op.cit. P. 17
143. Ibid.
144. Francke, A.H.; In : 'Encyclopaedia of Tibet', Op.cit., P. 111
145. Ibid.
146. Ibid., P. 112
147. Lha-chen-shesrab : Lhachen-shes-rab established Sabu village near Leh.
148. Sabu village : It is located at six miles south-east of Leh.
149. Francke, A.H.; In 'Encyclopaedia of Tibet', Op.cit., P. 113
150. Cf. Francke, A.H., In : 'Encyclopaedia of Tibet', P. 113. About the chortens, Francke says : "These rows of chortens, which were the forerunners of the mani-walls of which we shall hear on, usually consist of chortens not higher than two or three feet and in their dilapidated condition resemble low walls, built at random anyhow across the desert. But

those built by kings are at least six feet high. Of these at Sabu there is still a fragment left, of about six yards, It looks as if the other portion of it had been carried away by a flood." Cf. Francke, A.H.; 'Encyclopaedia of Tibet', Op. cit., P. 113

151. Spituk = dPe-t'ub

152. Vries, Sjoerd - Jande; Op.cit. P. 31

153. Petech; Op.cit. P. 166

154. dGe-lugs-pa order = Yellow school

155. Petech; Op.cit. P. 168

156. Nawang Tsering Shaskpo; PP. 18-19. The three Maitreya statues were popularly known byams-ba-rnam-gsum.

157. Tsoṅ-k'a-pa : (= Tsongkapa): Cf. Ref. No. 127

158. Tsogchen : The main assembly hall of the monastery.

159. Shes-rab-bzang-po : He was born at stagmo near Thikse. Cf. Nawang Tsering Shakspo; Op.cit., P. 19 & Kachen Lobzang Zodpa and Nawang Tsering Shakspo : 'Zans-dkar-gyi-rgyal-rabs-dang-chos-byung', 1979.

160. Nawang Tsering Shakspo; Op. cit., P. 19.

161. Petech; Op.cit., P. 23; Cf. Nawang Tsering Shaskpo Op.cit., P. 21

162. Nawang Tsering Shakspo; Op.cit., P. 21

163. Ibid., P. 22

164. Tashi Namgyal (= bKa-sis-rnam-rgyal) : According to Petech, King Tashi Namgyal Patronized 'Bri-guṅ-pa order in Ladakh and laid down the rule that every family of more than one male child had to give up one, not the eldest however, to become a lama. Thus he forced every family to offer one or more male child to the monasteries of 'Bri-guṅ-pa order and enrich this school in Ladakh. Cf. Petech, Luciano; Op.cit., P. 168.

165. Jamyang-Namgyal = 'Jam-dbyaṅs-rnam-rgyal : After the death of King Ts'e-dbaṅ-rnam-rgyal, all the vassal princes in one place after another rose and tried to declare independent kingdom. For example Ts'e-riṅ Malik of Cig-tan attached upon Purig. Latter 'Jam-dbyaṅs-rnam-rgyal got success to ascend the throne of Ladakh by his intelligent tactics and intervened to stop the battle between Ts'e-riṅ Malik of Cig-tan and prince of Purig. But King 'Jan-dyaṅs-ram-rgyal could not able to solve it easily and had to involve with his full army against the chief of Skardo Ali Mir's army. But lost the war and thrown into prison. When King agreed to marry with rGyal khatun, he was released. Thereafter King spent his latter days for religious works. Here follows the genealogy of the rnam-rgyal dyansty of Ladakh during 16th Century.

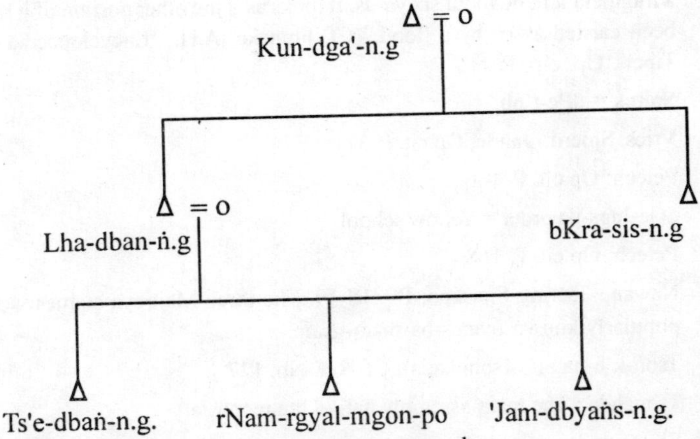

Note : n.g = rnam-rgyal

166. Stag-ts'aṅ-ras-pa (= sTag-ts'aṅ-ras-pa Ṅag-rgya-mts'o (1574-1651)) : He was a scion of the 'K' on family (i.e. of the house of the Sa-skya prince-abbots), and an outstanding member of the 'Brug-pa sect. He became a devoted pupil of Lha-rtse-ba Ṅag-dbaṅ-bzaṅ-po (1546-1615), the first Yoṅs-dzon incarnate of bDe-C'en-'K'or or monastery near Goṅ-dKar-rdzoṅ in central Tibet, who took a keen interest in western Tibet and whos successors became hereditary preceptors (*dbu-bla*) to the Ladakhi Kings. Lha-rtse-ba laid upon him the task of spreading the 'Brug-pa persuasion in Western Tibet; and he remembered and observed this command during the whole of his life. sTag-ts'aṅ-ras-pa travelled widely in Central and Eastern Tibet, as far as the sacred Wu-tai-shan mountain in China. Then in 1613 he started upon his great journey to Uḍḍiyāna (= Udyana or modern Swat). On his way out he visited Zangskar (Zaṅs-dkar) upon the invitation of bDe-ba-rgya-mts'o, a famous *siddha* belonging to the Southern (Bhutanese) branch of the 'Brug-pa and founder (in 1618) of 'Bar-gdan, the main monastery of Zangskar. When he received the message from King 'Jam-dbyaṅs-rnam-rgyal to visit Ladakh, he turned down the invitation for the moment being, as he had not yet accomplished the journey to Uddiyāna enjoined upon him by his master. Cf. Petech, Luciano; Op.cit., P. 35

167. Nawang Tsering Shakspo; Op.cit., P. 26

168. Mangtro monastery : It is also known as Thupten Shaling Chokhor. Sakya Scholar Dorje Palsang when arrived in Ladakh from Tibet, he went for meditationin a cave located at the present site of the monastery. As King Gras-'bum-lde came to know about him, called upon him to consecrate a new temple of Sakya order. As an offering for this service, the King

bestowed upon him a large tract of land. Upon this land Dorje Palsang decided to build a monastery for the benefit of the local community. This monastery latter known Mongtro monastery.

169. Yellow Sect : Lamas of this sect wear yellow Cap during ritual ceremonies

170. Vries, Sjoerd - Jan de; Op.cit., P.31

171. Sen-gey-rnam-gyal (= Seṅ-ge-rnam-rgyal) : After the death of King Jamyang-Namgyal, rGyal khatun carried on the government on behalf of her elder son Seṅ-ge-rnam-rgyal, apparently till then he was minor. Latter he became King of Ladakh and according to his nature extended his territory considerably. He handled the economic situation of Ladakh intelligently and established social and cultural harmony. In fact by his remarkable role for the propogation of Buddhism and handling the cultural and economic situation of Ladakh his reign is known as a 'golden period' of Ladakh.

172. sTag-ts'aṅ-ras-pa : When sTag-ts'aṅ-ras-pa first time visited Ladakh Jamyang-Namgyal was the King and his son Seṅ-ge-rnam-rgyal was minor. In his first visit he came Ladakh from Udyana via Kashmir and Zangskar. It is said that when he approaching to Leh, at first stayed at rGya as the guest of the local chiefs (*jo-ba*), who were supporters of the 'Brug-pa sect; one of the family, *druṅ-pa* bDe-ba, had been a pupil of Padma-dKar-po. As his fame spread, he was invited to K'rig-se and to S'el (Leh). At S'el he stayed at the palace where secondary queen Ts'e-riṅ with her sons acted as hosts. Then he went to Ba-sgo, where he was honoured by rGyal.Khatun and her son Seṅ-gernam-rgyal. Cf. Petech, L; Op.cit., P. 38

173. Nawang Tsering Shakspo; Op.cit. P. 38

174. Patech, L.; Op.cit., P.52

175. In 1622 wehen sTag-ts'aṅ-ras-pa returned to Ladakh, he came to know that late King Jamyang-namgyal (= 'Jam-dbyaṅs-rnam-rgyal) had undertaken to erect a large statue of Maitreya, but was not able to carry out his purpose, so in order to carry forward dead ruler he convinced the royal family to put forward the half done wishes of late King Jamyang-Namgyal. Thus the work began on the 19th October, 1622, the dowager queen Khatun supplied more than 500 ounces (*Źo*) of gold and gems of less values, and finally clay, copper and gilt mixed three stories high stone of Maitreya was being made in the Ba-sgo monastery. Cf. Petech, L. Op.cit., P. 40.

176. Nawang Tsering, Shakspo; Op.cit., P. 26.

177. Francke, A.H. : 'Antiquities of Indian Tibet', Op.cit., P. 57.

178. Petech, L; Op.cit., P. 55

179. Bdel-dan Namgyal (= bDe-ldan rNam-rgyal) : Like his father seṅ-ge-rnam-rgyal, he fought bravely against his opponents and extended his kingdom upto Zoji-la pass near Srinagar.

180. Chang-chub chorten : Bodhi Chorten (Stupa) : It was first time constructed when Buddha got enlightenment under Bodhi tree. It was constructed by King Bimbisar. Cf. Tsering Sonam (Tr. Prem sing Jina) an unpublished paper.

181. Nawang Tsering Shaskpo; Op.cit., PP. 29-30

182. Bdelegs - Namgyal (= Bde-legs-rnam-rgyal) : His whole period spent in war with Dga-'ldan-tshe-dbang. Finally when he took help from Moghals, won war against Dga-'ldan tshe-dbang. But had to sacrifice his religion and accepted Islam.

183. Nima-Namgyal (= Ṅi-ma-rnam-rgyal) : He occupies a special place among the Kings of Ladakh because of his activity in the field of justice. He appointed elders (*rgan-po*) for each district to decide questions. Legal documents (*bKa'-S'og*) concerning matters of landed property. Thus he never gave his judgment without consulting his state officers. Cf. Petech, L.; Op.cit. P. 83.

184. mK'ar - rtse (= Ka-ja). It is in Spiti, now in Himachal Pradesh.

185. Petech, L : Op.cit. P. 85

186. Bar-gdan monastery : It is situated at the 12 kms. south of Padum. This monastery belongs to 'Brug pa order of having 40 monks. It was founded during 17th century as the first ever centre of the old, unreformed 'Brug-pa monastic order in Zangskar. Of course Bar-gdan monastery in Zangskar is a head of all 'Brug-pa order of other small establishment. This monastery has a large assembly hall around which all other structures are organized, contains beautiful statues of Buddhist divinities and small stupas in clay, bronze, wood and copper. Perched atop a rocky crag, rising vertically from the Lungnak river bed. Cf. Ladakh : Kargil & Zangskar; Op.cit. P. 28

187. rDzong-khul monastery (= Zangkhul monastery) Cf. Ref. No. 114

188. Nawang Tsering : 'Buddhism in Ladakh', Op. Cit. P. 41

189. Petech, L.; Op.cit., P.101

190. Nawang Tsering Shakspo; Op.cit. P. 37

191. Hemis festival (= Hemis Tseshu)

192. Nawang Tsering Shakspo; Op.cit., P. 38

193. Petech, L. : Op.cit., P. 120

194. Tsetan Namgyal : He was the elder son Tsewang Namgyal II. He was diligent, and obtained proficiency in Tibetan grammar and mathematics, Persian letters and speech, Kashmiri speech, and other such languages. He also knew well how to govern. His ability was evidenced in his regulation of the taxes. He died in his twenty-fourth year at Leh. Cf. Francke, A.H. : 'The Last two Kings, about 1780-1834'; In : 'Encyclopaedia of Tibet; Op.cit. 126.

195. Francke, A.H. : 'The Last Two Kings, about 1780-1834', In : Encyclopaedia of Tibet, Op.cit., P. 126.

196. Ibid; P. 128
197. Petech, L.; Op.cit., P.132
198. Vries, Sjoerd-Jan de; Op.cit., P.31
199. Shankar = bSam-dKar : It is a sub gompa of dGe-lugs-pa under dPe-thub monastery
200. dges-bśes : It is Buddhist philosophy degree of traditional Buddhist education equivalent to Ph.D. degree.
201. Vries, Sjoerd-Jande; Op.cit., P.34
202. bla-brangs : Lamas 'residence
203. Nawang Tsering Shakspo; Op.cit., P. 50
204. Earlier Maharaja donated 24 Kannals land for the constructed of a *gompa* in Srinagar, but in 1960 it was reduced to only one kannal (one Kannal = 5,440 sq. feet), Cf. Nawang Tsering Shakspo; Op.cit., P.51
205. Buddhist delegation had the following members :
   (i) Bakula Rin-po-che
   (ii) Gergan konchog Sonam
   (iii) Lama Kunga

   The Buddhist delegation fight against state Abolition Act because all monasteries had large land and there was possibility to cease their land by the State government.
206. Nawang Tsering Shakspo; Op.cit., PP. 54-61.
207. Ibid. P.62
208. Mani-dung-'phur : The recitation of millions of Mani-mantras
209. Nawang Tsering Shakspo; Op.cit., P.63
210. Jivetsal : It is a compound at Choglamsar village near Leh.
211. Menon,Appan; 'Lessons from Ladakh', Frontline, July 28-August, 1989, PP. 15-16
212. Ibid & Booklet on 'Ladakh : People movement for Union Territory Status'.
213. Booklet on 'Ladakh : Peoples movement for Union Territory status', Op.cit.
214. Ibid.
215. Menon, Appan; Op.cit.
216. Nawang Tsering, Op.cit., P.64
217. Booklet on 'Ladakh : Peoples movement for Union Territory Status', Op.cit.
218. Ibid.
219. Menon, Appan; Op.cit.

220. ladags Melong; No.1, 1993; P.6

221. Ibid.; P.7

222. "Advisery Council for Leh announced', the Tribune, Tuesday, 15th May, 1995, P.16.

223. Ladages Melong, Vol. I, 1995, P.11

224. Ibid, 1996, PP.22-23

225. Ibid., 1997, P.5

Chapter - III
ISLAM IN LADAKH

Prem Singh Jina & Zain-ul-Abidin

Early Muslim Traders

During a visit to Chang-thang region in 1993 Dr. Prem Singh Jina acknowledged some old inscriptions of Sogdian language on high boulders near Tangtse. According to him during $4^{th} - 10^{th}$ Century many merchants from Samarkand used to come to Western Tibet for trade. Some of them even came up to Tangtse. Besides others, Muslim traders were in large number. Thus they frequently visited during summers at the higher altitudes plains like Tangtse, Rudok etc. till the end of 10th Century. But after the collapse of the Tibetan monarchy, Ladakh was deeply influenced by Tibetanization and Muslim traders could not get time to extend trade activity in Ladakh. Finally unable to influence Ladakhis by Islam.

Islam during Grags-'bum-lde period

King Grags-'bum-lde was religious man. He patronized Buddhism and built many Buddhist temples in Ladakh. But as Islam brought to Western Himalayas by Kashmiri Sultans, Ladakh also effected. Under the Holy War - *Jihād* Baltistan was the first target. During 14th Century Muslim force from Kashmir crossed Zoji-La and invaded Baltistan under the leadership of Rai Madari. Petech explains :

"The conversion of Kashmir to Islam brought a new element of instability to Western Himalayas, because of imperialistic trends of some of the Kashmiri Sultans, under the mantle of the Holy War (*jihād*) against the infields. Their first target was Baltistan, which the Kashmiris called Little Tibet, while Ladakh was called Great Tibet. The first Muslim force from Kashmir to cross to Zoji-la and to invade the country beyond the pass was led by Rai Madari, in the reign of Sikandar (1394-1416). He conquered Baltistan and under unknown circumstances Baltistan and Purig were converted to Islam."[1]

Immediately after the above success, Sultan Zain-ul-Abidin[2] led an expedition against Tibet, Raja of Baltistan was also with him. Sultan Zain-ul-Abidin's intension was to in invade Gu-ge and propogate Islam in Ladakh and Gu-ge. Accordingly he came to Ladakh and stayed at Sheh.[3] King Grags-'bum-lde warmly welcomed him and his army. He had made all necessary arrangements for them and gave VIP treatment to Sultan Zain-ul-Abidin who stayed as a King's guest at Sheh palace. As Sultan of Kashmir stayed a long period, so, he called his Muslim leaders at Sheh palace and asked them to propogate Islam in Ladakh. King 'Bum-lde of Ladakh came to know about the Islamic activities in Ladakh, but he did not make any objection. Thus Islam spread its roots in Ladakh peacefully. Petech says :

"Sultan Zain-ul-Abidin led personally an expedition against Tibet and plundered the country and massacred the people, on this occasion Ladakh too was invaded. It seems that Sheh was sacked in the course of the invasion, as the King saved a golden statue of the Buddha from the hands of his soldiers in Śayadeśa. Of course Zain-ul-Abidin intended no permanent conquest; it was merely one of the customary raids aimed at collecting plunder and extorting tribute."[4]

Muslim Invasion at the last of 15th Century

During 15th Century nothing much could be done by the Kashmiri Sultans in the propogation of Islam in its neighbouring this Century in 1483 Sultan Shāh[5] sent Jahāngīr Magre and Sayyid Hasan to invade Little and Great Tibet.[6] Sayyid Hasan went to Baltistan and Jahāngīr entered Ladakh, but were defeated. Therefore, Muslim invaders did not do much in the propogation of Islam in Ladakh.

Mīrzā Haidar Dughlāt and Islam

Mīrzā Haidar Dughlāt[7] invaded Ladakh and Tibet respectively during King Blo-gros-mt'og-ldan in the 15th Century. When Haidar arrived at Leh, King of ladakh Blo-gros welcomed him and provided all necessary facilities during his stay at Sheh palace. Mīrzā Haidar stayed for several months in Ladakh and asked Ladakhis who came in contact to follow Islam. According to Petech :

"King Blo-gros-mc'og-ldan (or Blo-gros-mt'-og-ldan) of the 15th century apparently, managed to maintain friendly relations with the invaders occupying his country. After some time Mīrzā Haidar invaded Tibet. But the climate and terrific difficulties of the terrain stood against the invaders as a barrier more formidable than any Tibetan army; and the Mīrzā had to turn back when he was at eight days march from Ursang (Lhasa). He reached safely Ladakh, and retired to Sheh, where to stayed for two years more, in 1536 he departed for Badakhsa."[8]

After staying a few years in Badakhsa he marched towards Kashmir and became the ruler of Kashmir, but did not forget his earlier venture to capture Ladakh and Tibet. Subsequently, in 1545 he invaded Ladakh, but could not get major success. In 1548 he launched a large-scale operation. This time he got success, annexed Ladakh and Beltistan with Kashmir. To lookafter the administration of these regions he appointed his governors Mullah Qasim for Batistan and Mullah Hasan for Ladakh.[9]

Some more invasion from Kashmir

Mīrzā Haidar was a terrific man, he forcefully asked Ladakhis to embrace Islam. After Mīrzā the other invaders from Kashmir were not much effective. Among them were Daulat Chak, Sankar Chak, Ibrahim Chak, Haidar Chak etc. Therefore, during Mīrzā Haidar invasion to till 1560 Ladakh was not allowed to enjoy peace and harmony.[10]

Kashmiri and Hor Invation

In 1562 King Ghazi Chak invaded Ladakh under the command of Ahmad Khan and Fath Chak. Fath Chak came up to the capital of Ladakh, but returned after a promise of tribute. After sometimes Hor forces[11] invaded Ladakh, King of Ladakh this time fought bravely and killed many of them as a result they could not enter further in Ladakh and returned.[12]

'Jam-dbyaṅs-rnam-rgyal (Jamyang-Namgyal) and Islam

When 'Jam-dbyaṅs-rnam-rgyal ascended the throne two chiefs – Ts'e-riṅ Malik of Cig-tan and another chief of Purig started quarrelling with each other. The new King therefore immediately decided to solve the problem in Lower Ladakh and departured to Purig with his army. His presence provoked the intervation of Ali Mir.[13] Thereafter direct war between Ladakh and Balti chief Ali Mir army took place. King lost the battle and surrendered before the Balti army. He was carried to Skardo. King 'Jam-dbyaṅs-rnam-rgyal though sent to prison, yet he was given royal treatment, latter after meeting with Yabgo Sher Ghaze, Ali Mir agreed to release Jamyang Namgyal from prison under the following conditions that – King Jamyang Namgyal will have to marry with Yabgo Sher Ghaze's daughter rGyal-Khatun; rGyal-Khatun's son will be the next King of Ladakh and King Jamyang Namgyal should give proper shelter to Islam in Ladakh. King Jamyag Namgyal accepted the above conditions. He married with rGyal Khatun and returned to his Kingdom alongwith rGyal Khatun. Latter on the request of rGyal Khatun Ali Mir sent some Balti musicians, Akhons and others to perform Muslim rituals and entertainment. These Balti Muslims latter settled down in Phyang and along Indus belt and, propogated Islam in Ladakh.

bDe-ldan-rnam-rgyal (Bdel-dan-Namgyal) and Islam

It is said that during Seṅ-ge-rnam-rgyal when King fought against Mughals and the war came to end after an agreement under which King promised to pay tribute to the Mughals. But his tribute was never paid. Later during bDe-ldan-rnam-rgyal when Emperor Aurangzeb sent his envoys to Ladakh to remind the payment of tribute. Like his father he promised to pay tribute and according to the wishes of Emperor he would build a mosque and circulate coins in the name of Emperor. However, as soon as emperor envoys returned Kashmir he did nothing. In 1665, the governor of Kashmir, sent an envoy to the King of Ladakh this time envoy, Muhammad Sharif carried *farmān*, enjoining on the Ladakhi King the acceptance of Mughal suzerainty and of Islam and threatening him with an invasion by imperial army in case of refusal. Accordingly, the *Khutba* was read on behalf of Aurangzeb, the foundation of a mosque was laid, king patronized Islam in his Kingdom and gave tribute of 1000 *ashrafis* to the envoy. Thereafter he returned to Kashmir with great honour.[14]

bDe-legs-rnam-rgyal (Bdelegs Namgyal) and Islam

In 1680 Dga'-ldan-ts'e-dbaṅ along his 5000 men attacked Ladakh. He easily defeated Ladakhi army at all fronts and reached Leh. Later he occupied Leh without encountering resistance. Then Ladakhi army entrenched themselves near Ba-sgo and King resided at sTiṅ-mosgaṅ (Timosgang). This time they faced Mongols bravely and fighting continued for three years (1581-1663). At last Ladakhi King sent his envoy to Kashmir and asked Ibrahim Khan, the Mughal governor of Kashmir[15] to intervine and help him. He sent a small army under Fidai Khan which was later reinforced by troops from Baltistan and entered Lower ladakh and attacked Tibeto-Mongols from sNe-mo (Nimo)[16] side mountains. Mongols were defeated. Faidai Khan then submitted some conditions. To pay tribute which was due since 1664 and to accept Islam and promise to propogate Islam in his Kingdom.[17]

Relations with the Muslim chieftains

King Ṅi-ma-rnam-rgyal (or Nima-Namgyal) (1691-1695) like his father maintained good relations with the Mughals emperor. In those days Ladakh received good revenue from the traders who passed through Ladakh towards Central

Asian countries. Keeping in view King restored the trade via Ladakh to Yarkand and other Central Asian countries. Thus Kashmiri muslim merchants started trade activities. On the way to leh they stayed at the *Sarais* provided by Ladakh government. During the course of their stay at the villages of Ladakh they got the chance to marry with Ladakhi Buddhist girls. These temporary marriages helped them to propogate Islam in Ladakh. Besides Ladakhi Kings in many occasions asked for help by the neighbouring Muslim cheifs. Which strengthen the Islamic activities in Ladakh. Here follows the details.

1. Ṅi-ma-rnam-rgyal (Nima Namgyal) married a lady from Balti chief family of Ka-pu-lu. The name of lady was Zi-zi Khatun. In 1716 when quarrels started between S'i-sgar and Skardo. Ladakhi forces went S'i-sgar. This time Ladakhi forces went Skardo via Hanu and normalized the situation.[18]
2. In 1722 Azam Khan, the chief of S'i-sgar wished to extend his kingdom to whole of Baltistan. Hatim Khan of K'a-pu-lu came to know Azam Khan's intention and asked help from Ladakh. The King of Ladakh then sent his general Ts'ul-k'rims-rdo-rje via Nubra to K'a-pu-lu and defeated Azam Khan. Later Ladakhis installed Ali-Khan as the new chief of S'i-sgar, and Mahmud Zafar Khan as Duke of Skardo.[19]
3. In 1759 when S'i-sgar chief Husain Khan was taken prisoner by Skardo ruler Muhammad Zafar Khan, Mir Beg of keris made preparation to attack K'a-pu-lu. Mahmud Ali Khan then the chief of K'a-pu-lu, as usual he applied for help from Ladakh. The Ladakhi army marched ahead under the command of No-no dBaṅ-rgyal and No- no Ṅag-dbaṅ. They fought bravely and Skardo forces who were also involved is this battle, thrown back. Subsequently Husain Khan was liberated. Peace agreement was signed which followed for many years on the Balti frontier.[20]
4. About 1760 or so a Muslim trader called Mirza Malik influenced a lot the King of Ladakh. He had about highbred Central Asian horses. His friends were mostly Muslims. Therefore, King inclined towards Islam.[21]
5. After the death of King bKra-śis-rnam-rgyal of Purig in 1759 his Kingdom annexed to Ladakh. Later in 1773 or perhaps during the last period of King Ts'e-dbaṅ-rnam-rgyal reign, Shia sect being favoured by King of Ladakh.[22]
6. In 1785 S'i-sgar and Skardo chiefs declared war; they put a large force in the field and built a fortress at Balaghar. They took the

castles of Kye-ris and ku-re and prepared to attack the chief of K'a-pu-lu. Mahmud Ali Khan asked help from Ladakh. Ladakhi King sent Non-no bSod-nams-nor-bu with a small number of Ladakhi soldiers marched towards K'a-pu-lu via Nubra Valley. They defeated enemy at 'Dre-go-ni near K'a-pu-lu and restored the peace in the neighbouring Balti small countries.[23]

7. In 1792 A'zam Khan of S'i-sgar asked help from Ladakh. Ladakhi King sent his force under the command of Ts'e-dban-don-grub due to hot season the commander did not move after Purig.[24]
8. In 1804 under the direction of King of Ladakh, Ladakhi forces commanded by Ts'e-dban-don-grub against Muhammad Sultan who had seized S'i-dKar and won the war. In 1810 King issued a document at K'a-la-rtse refered to a siege of Śi-dKar by Ahmad shah. In 1811 again Ladakhi forces attack Balti forces. Ladakh troops merched towards K'a-pu-lu and got success in the mission. However, in 1812 trouble arose again at K'a-pu-lu. After the gap of only 3 years (i.e. in 1815) again conflict broke out with Ahmad Shah over the castle of sKye-ris. No-no rTa-mgrin-rnam-rgyal took the command of Ladakhi forces. Baltis were defeated.[25]

Thus viewing to the above facts it may rightly infer that the relations with the Muslim chieftain to the north-west were influenced the Ladakhi life, as such many Baltis time and again migrated to Ladakh and settled down in and around Indus belt. Some of them even married Ladakhi Buddhist women and slowly helped in the propogation of Islam in Ladakh.

After 1825 Ladakh entered into the political orbit of the Sikh Kingdom. Earlier Ranjit was not keen to annex Ladakh later situation changed and in 1834 Dogra army of Raja Gulab Singh of Jammu under the command of Zorawar Singh invaded Ladakh and annexed it with his Kingdom. In those days Ladakh was the centre of shawl wool which was imported here from Western Tibet later sold it to the merchants of Kashmir and Kullu. But during Dogra period (1834-40) the whole consignment of shawl wool was transit to Kashmiri merchants. These Kashmiri merchants were muslims who during summer came to Leh and often arranged temporary marriages with Ladakhi women. This tradition continued for many years and Kashmiri muslims enjoyed home atmosphere in Ladakh too. This also helped to propogate Islam and increase Muslim population in Leh district. Thus like Shia sect of Islam Sunni Sect also got favourable atmosphere in Ladakh.

Muslim monuments in Leh-Ladakh

1. **Khankana of Chuchot Yogma :** It was constructed during 16th

Century by Meer Shamsud-Din - Iraqi and his deciple Sayeed. They visited S'i-sgar, K'a-pu-lu and sKardo (Skardo) for the propogation of Islam there. Later after completing their mission in the above countries they turned towards Ladakh.

2. **Tsas Soma mosque :** In the middle of 16th Century King Ts'e-dbaṅ-rNam-rgyal when decided to shift his palace from Sheh to Leh, the Muslims also decided to construct Tsas Soma Mosque.

3. **Jama Masjid Ahli-Sunnati :** It is at Lal Chowk of Leh town. It is said that when Tibetan army under the command of dGa'-ldan-ts'e-dbaṅ invaded Ladakh. Ladakhi King bDe-legs-rnam-rgyal (Bdelegs Namgyal) then unable to fight against the Tibetan army. He, therefore, asked help from the Governor of Kashmir under Mughal Empire. The Mughal Governor accepted the request of Ladakhi King and sent Mughal army to Ladakh for help. Thereafter the joint force of Ladakh and Mughal soldiers defeated Tibetan army. But Mughal Governor put some terms and condition such as to construct Mosque in Ladakh and help in the propogation Islam in the Kingdom of Ladakh. Ladakhi King accepted these conditions and under the direction of Kashmir Governor Jama Masjid was constructed at Leh.

4. **Chutey Rantak mosque :** It was constcuted at Leh during Ladakhi King 'Jam-dbjaṅs-rnam-rgyal (Jamyang Namgyal) period.

5. **Mosque at Hunder :** The Hunder Mosque was constructed by the direction of queen rGyal Khatoon for her personal prayer. But this mosque washed away by flood at Dok Nallah in 1926.

6 **Mosque at Bazgo (Ba-sgo) :** Like Hunder Mosque, rGyal Khatoon when came to Bażgo, she ordered to construct a mosque at Bazgo for her personal prayer.

7. **Masjid Sharif and Imam Bara of Phyang :** When King 'Jam-dbyaṅs-rnam-rgyal (Jamyang Namgyal) was released by Ali Mir of Skardo alongwith his noble men and his new queen rGyal Khatoon; many Balti muslims also accompained him who later settled down at Phyang Village. Because they came Ladakh for the ritual purpose of queen rGyal Khatoon, therefore, queen on their request constructed a mosque at Phyang.

8. **Tyakshi mosque :** It is said during 14th Century when Shah Hamdani visited Tyakshi, he offered Namaj at the left side path to Tyakshi village. Later local inhabitants constructed mosque

at his memory.

9. **Turtuk mosque :** Dr. Jina visited Turtuk during 1998 and found that Turtuk mosque is one of the oldest mosque of Ladakh and contemporary to Tyakshi mosque.

Today Balti of Shia sect is dominant in Kargil district where it has eighty percent population. Besides one can notice their population throughout in Leh district. The following table shows the details.

Table : 3.1

Balti Muslims in Leh district of Ladakh

S.No.	Name of Village	Block
(1)	(2)	(3)
1.	Sheh	Leh
2.	Thiksey	Leh
3.	Rambirpura	Leh
4.	Chuchot-Gongma	Leh
5.	Chuchot-Shamma	Leh
6.	Chuchot-Yokma	Leh
7.	Leh	Leh
8.	Phyang	Leh
9.	Partapur	Nubra
10.	Diskit	Nubra
11.	Hunder	Nubra
12.	Bogdang	Nubra
13.	Choglamsar	Leh
14.	Housing colony	Leh
15.	Parchathang	Nubra
16.	Turtuk	Nubra
17.	Thang	Nubra
18.	Tyakshi	Nubra

However, there were some Muslim families in the following villages who later converted into Buddhism or migrated.

1.	Nimo (village)–	Leh (block)
2.	Durbuck (village)– & Tangtse	Leh (Durbuk blcok)

3.	Basgo (village)–	Khalsi block
4.	Zaffar pa (family)–	Leh district
5.	Samad pa (family)–	Leh district
6.	Qasum pa (family)–	Leh district
7.	Azimpa (family)–	Leh district
8.	Baltipa (family)–	Leh district
9.	Qurban pa (family)–	Leh district

Contribution of Akhons, Sheiks and Agas in the propogation of Islamic education in Ladakh

Akhons, Sheikhs and Agas of Shia Muslim families who perform Islamic religious principals, Hadeth, rituals and even preach the people of Quran teachings.

In the Muslim community Akhons are popularly known *Ulemas*. They are fully dedicated religious families who work to strengthen the roots of Islam in Ladakh. Some of the Akhon families are as under :

1. Akhon Mohsin of Chuchot Gongma
2. Akhon Mohammad of Chuchot Yokam
3. Akhon Fatahullah of Sheh
4. Akhon Assadullah of Thiksey
5. Akhon Ali of Phyang
6. Akhon Abdul Hussain of Leh
7. Akhon Ahamad Ali Leh.

It is difficult to trace the past history (i.e. before 17th Century) of Akhon families in Ladakh. Moreover, there is one Akhon family of Chuchot Gongma of Leh belongs to 18th Century. According to Akhon Mohammad Hussain, his great grandfather Baba Ali was Akhon of Chuchot Gongma and its neighbouring villages during 18th Century. He had good knowledge of Quran and expert in performing rituals. He was liberal minded and did not make any objection for drinking wine. As a result Balti Muslims often used chang or other intoxigated drinks on the occasion of Idd, Losar and other important festivals of Ladakh. Later his grandson Akhon Mohsin went Mecca for Haj. He was strict man and put restriction for the use of intoxigated drinks and other social evils which were then previlents in the Muslim society. Besides, he introduced Parda system according to the Shariat. Akhon Mohsin was first Haji from Ladakh. Here follows the lineage of his family.

Akhon Ali Baba

↓

Akhon Ghulam Ali

↓

Alhaj Akhon Mohsin
(Chuchot Gongma)

↓

Akhon Fida Hussain

↓ ↓

Alhaj Sheikh Mohammad Hadi | Akhon Mohammad Hussain

Sheikh Mohammad Hadi is a great scholar of Islamic religion. he got religion education from Najaf Iraq. Now Arabic teacher and performs religious duties.

Sheikh Mirza Mehdi

He belongs to Chuchot Yogma of Leh district. The lineage of his family can be traced up to four generations.

Sheikh Mirza Mehdi's great grand father was Akhon Abdul Hassan, his son was Akhon Mohammad and grandson Akhon Mohammad Ali were very much inclined towards Islam and devoted their whole life in strengthening the roots of Shia Islam in the Indus belt of Ladakh during fifties of eighteenth and nineteenth centuries. They were the custodian of Khankana and Immambarah of Chuchot Yogma village for long period.

The great grand son of Akhon Abdul Hassan is Sheikh Mirza Mehdi. He got Islamic education from Najaf Ashraf, Iraq. At present he is working as Arabic teacher. Here follows the details about his ancestors :

Akhon Abdul Hassan

↓

Akhon Mohammad

↓

Akhon Mohammad Ali

↓

Akhon Abdul Hamid

↓

Sheikh Mirza Mehdi

Akhon Mohammad

He belongs to Chuchot Yogma. His family had valuable contribution in the propogation of Islam in Ladakh. The family history of Akhon Mohammad is as follows : During forties of 19th Century cho Ghulam Khan, son in law of cho Rahim Khan of Chuchot was a knight or (Cho) and an influential personality of his time. He was a great warrior and commander of Zorawar's expedition to Baltistan and Tibet during 1840-42. After Zorawar Singh's death he was taken to Tibet as a prison of war. Later he married with Tibetan girl and never returned. Before Dogra war Cho Ghulam Khan married with a girl from Chuchot Village near Leh, he had a daughter Amina Khatoon from her. Who later married with Akhon Mohammad of Kanor, Kargil district. Akhon Mohammad as said earlier was a religious man and devoted his whole life in the propogation of Islam in Ladakh. The following members of his family like him educated in Iraq and serving muslim community as religious heads :

1. Sheikh Mohammad Ali Akhonpa
2. Sheikh Toha Akhonpa
3. Sheikh Ghulam Abbas
4. Sheikh Ghulam Mohammad Akhon

The following chart shows the further details

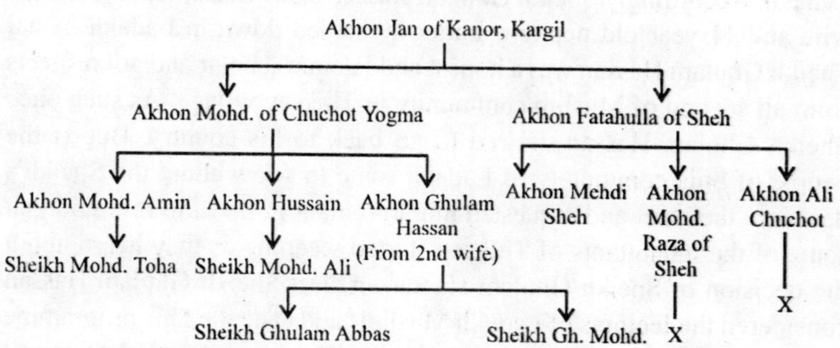

Akhon Ali of Phyang

Akhon Ali was religious head of Balti muslims at Phyang. He taught Islamic teachings to the people of Phyang. The lineage of his family is shown below :

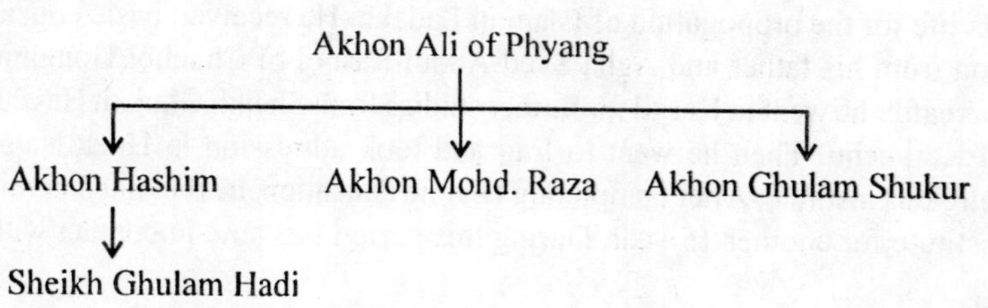

Akhon Abdul Hussain

He was the grandfather of late Akbar Ladakhi who was the richest man of Balti Muslim community in Ladakh. He contributed his services in the preservation and promotion of Islamic in Ladakh. Besides he helped in the establishment of Maktabas and organised *Majilisi* Hussani in Leh. Under his supervision Imambara of Leh was shifted to Leh town. He first time organised *Majlis* and started procession through the main Leh *bazar*.

When Akhon Abdul Hussain was fully convinced by the function of Leh Immambara during Moharram days, he decided to go Mecca for *Haj*. Later along with *Haji* Mohd. Taqi and *Haji* Issa Ali Zimskang of Churchot he went to Mecca and Najaf for *Haj* and *Ziarat*. There he met Sheikh Ghulam Hassan of Baltistan who was studying at Najaf, Iraq. He was a simple and religious man Akhon Abdul Hussain was very much impressed by his religious teachings, latter invited him Ladakh for religious purpose.

Sheikh Ghulam Hassan

He belonged to Pari Kharmang Baltistan and got religious education from Najaf, Iraq. After completing Islamic education from Najaf, he came to Huza Ilmia Najaf, where he met Akhon Abdul Hussain who invited him to Ladakh. Accordingly Sheikh Ghulam Hassan came Ladakh alongwith his wife and 11 year old nephew. Latter he settled down in Ladakh. Alhaj Sheikh Ghulam Hassan was a honest and Islamic scholar and got respects from all section of Muslim community in Thiksey village. As such once Sheikh Ghulam Hassan desired to go back to his country. But as the people of Shia community of Ladakh came to know about the Sheikh's decision, they met and requested him to remain in Ladakh. It is said that some of the inhabitants of Thiksey started weeping as they heard about the decision of Sheikh Ghulam Hassan. At last Sheikh Ghulam Hassan considered the feelings of Ladakh Muslims and cancelled his programme to return to Baltistan. Thereafter he came to Thiksey and settled down and continued his services for the development of Islam in Ladakh.

Sheikh Mohammad Ali Zubdavi

He was the son of Sheikh Ghulam Hassan. Like his father he devoted his life for the propogation of Islam in Ladakh. He received basic education from his father and Agha Syed Abdul Rasool of Chuchot Gongma, thereafter he went to Kargil for further studies from Sheikh Ghulam Hassan of Karkechu. Then he went to Iraq and took admission in Huza Najaf religious institute. After completing Islamic education, he remained in this institute for another 15 year. During this period he came in contact with

Agha Shahrudi and Agha Khoi R.A. Subsequently after receiving of Darsi kharij, he returned Ladakh in 1965. At present he is the President of Majlesi Ulema Leh and performing the duties of Prayer leader (Imami Juma) at Imamia Jama Masjid Leh.

Agha Syed Abdul Rasool

He served the religious duties for Shia Muslim community of yarkand and Ladakh during 1940 to 1960. It is said that Syed Tusab Shah and Syed Najaf Shah were well known traders of Central Asia in 1940. They had trade link with Yarkand and Chinese Turkestan. In those days many Shia Muslim traders settled down in Yarkand but did not have any such person who could perform religious duties rightly or act as shia Ulema. Therefore, in order to perform such duties according to the Shia Isna Ashri tradition in Yarkand, Syed Turab Shah invited Agha Shyed Abdul Rasool in Yarkand. Thereafter Agha Shyed Adbul visited Yarkand and served the Muslim community. He stayed several years in Yarkand, but returned to Ladakh with the intention to go to Kashmir.

It is said that when Agha Shyed arrived in Ladakh a delegation of Shia Muslims from Chuchot village met him at Leh and requested him to stay in Ladakh as religious leader. Thereafter keeping the demand of Shia muslims of Ladakh he decided to remain in Ladakh and serve for them. In his last days he settled down in Chuchot Gongma village and passed away in 1960.

Agha Syed Mohammad

He is the son of Agha Syed Abdul Rasool. Like his father he is a good scholar of Islamic Philosophy. He got religious education from Huza Ilmia Njaf institute, Iraq. Nowadays he is running an Islamic school of Shia sect in Srinagar. This school is located at Gund Hasi bat. The name of school is "Huza Imani Raza" and is popular among Ladakhi Balti students. During Moharram and Asad he annually visits Ladakh and address the religious gathering in Leh.

Besides, some layman also helped in the propogation of Islam in Ladakh. Here follows the details :

Syed Turab Shah

He was a businessman of post independance period of Ladakh. He alongwith his companion Akhon Abdu and Syed Najaf Shah helped a lot in the upliftment of Shia muslim in Ladakh. He promoted religions education among the muslims and encouraged them to open Maktabas in every villages. He opened a private school –

"Imamia School" at Chutey Rantag in Leh. It was the first private school in Leh, which was opened in post independence period by a Shia muslim. But it could not smoothly run due to financial crises. However, many important personalities got their basic education from this school, popular among them are : Late Akbar Ladakhi, Munshi Mohammad Baquir, Syed Ali Sha, Munshi Issa etc.

Haji Ghulam Haidi

He was Jamadar in Tehsil office Leh during post independence period. During Indo-Pak work in 1947-48 he worked as laison officer and was responsible to arrange labours and ponies for Indian army later devoted his life for religious activities.

Munshi Ali Hussain

He was the son of a noble family of Chuchot Gogma, popularly known pony track engineer. He constructed many pony tracks and foot paths in Leh district. The old Tulum poti track among Ladakhis is still popular. There are many folk songs in Ladakh which belong to him. In one Ladakhi folk song the importance of Tulum poti track is described. Thus this track undoubtly very useful for horse riders.

Haji Akhon Mohd. Hussain Abidi

He was the son of Haji Ali Mir Abidi, Kharmang of Baltistan and settled down in Thiksey village of Leh district. It is said that his ancestors were having various occupations at the ancient Bhoti cho palace of Pari. They were holding posts like Kharpons of Ladakhi *Rajas*. The orchards and fields of the surrounding of the above palace is still under the occupation of his brother Gh. Abbas Abidi and other relatives.

Haji Akhon Mohd. Hussain came Ladakh at the age of 11 alongwith his relative Sheikh Ghulam Hassan Zubdavi and father of Imani Juma Sheikh Mohd. Ali Zubdari of Thiksey and remained in Ladakh after partition.

Haji Akhon Mohd. Hussain Abidi migrated Ladakh from Baltistan, he got primary education from Kharmang, Baltistan, later arrived in Ladakh and studied Islamic education under the guidance of Sheikh Ghulam Hassan Zubdavi of Thiksey. He also learnt Persian, Urdu, Yarkandi, Balti and Tibetan language. As a poet he composed dozens of Qasidas and Naat Sharif in Balti languages. He had been recognised as a good Orator. Not only this his speeches were very impressive. In 1974 he dilivered speech in presence of Shaikh Moh. Abdullah, K.G. Bakula, Kashmiri leaders and others. The present auidance then were very much influenced and praised his scholarly speech.

Haji Akhon Mohd. Hussain Abidi was a trader and engaged in supplying goods to the remote parts of Chang-thang region. After 1962 Indo-China war, he could not continue his trade. Thereafter, he decided to come in politics and, worked sincerely for the welfare of Ladakhis under the leadership of Rev-K. G. Bakula.

Late Sonam Wangyal, when became Minister of Jammu and Kashmir State Government he was holding two posts of Congress party at Leh–Chief Organiser and Gernal Secretary of District Congress Committee. He was bold and fearless person and always ready to work for the communal harmony.

In 1982 struggle of Scheduled Tribe status for Ladakhis, he was sent to jail for 40 days alongwith other Ladakhi leaders viz. Tsering Samphel, P.T. Wangyal, Norboo Gyaltsan, Nisar Hussain and Tashi Targes Dimbir. Later when Gulham Sha's party came in power at the State all the above Ladakhis were released from the Leh prision.

On 18th Spetember 1994 Alhaj Akhon Mohd. Hussain passed away at the age of 72 and was burried at the grave yard of Thiksey.

Qadir Ali of Sheh

He was well known Hakim of Ladakh. According to Ali Hussain of Sheh, Qadir Ali's grandfather Momin Ali was the first Muslim Hakim in Leh district. He learned this noble profession from a Baltistani Hakim and got training under the guidance of Lharjey Gh. Mohd. Later he started medical practice at Sheh village. He like his ancestors prepared medicine powder and tablets from the local harbal plants. Sometimes he had to import valuable herbs from the other countries.

Thus Qadir Ali served to people honestly and gave medical treatment to all people without the bar of caste, colour and religion. He was a religious person and gave his full support in the religious activities. Finally in 1963 he passed away.

Mohd. Sharif

He was the son of Qadir Ali. Like his father he also followed the same method of medical treatment. He was very much popular among Muslims. Patients came to him for medical treatment from Leh and Kargil districts. By nature he was simple and honest person. He helped religious activities and inspired the people to follow Islamic principles.

Amchi Mohd. Sharif passed away on February 1996 at the age of 60 years and burried at Sheh village. After his death Amchi practice system did not follow by any Muslim for a long period. However, Mohd. Afzal decided to continue his ancestoral Amchi profession. The lineage of his family is as follows :

Amchi Momin Ali
↓
Ghulam Mohd. (Amchi)
↓
Amchi Qadir Ali
↓
Amchi Mohd. Sharif
↓
Mohd. Afzal
(Doing Amchi training)

Mohd. Akbar Ladakhi

He was the son of Chodhry Gh. Mohd. and grand son of Akhon Abdul Hussain. It is said that his grandfather Akhon Abdul Hussain came Ladakh from Baltistan before Independece in connection with business, later permanantly settled down in Leh. His mother was from a respectable Buddhist family of Ayu Kalon of Sabu village. His father and fore father were richest person among the Muslim community of Ladakh. They extended their all sort of co-operation for organising Muharram procession and establishing Maktabas in different Muslim village.

Mohd. Akbar Ladakhi had received his basic education from Imamia Public School, Leh and Upper Primary education from Middle School, Leh. After passing matriculation from Ladakh he went to Srinagar and Lucknow for Higher education. He loved literature and read interestingly Balti language and Balti poetry. He was an active political leader and closely associated with Kh. Gh. Mohd. Sadiq. When G.M. Sadiq became the Chief Minister of Jammu & Kashmir state he was appointed Information Officer, later worked in different capacities till his retirement from the state Govt. service. He worked as S.D.M. Sopore, PRO to Sonam Narboo, Minister Public works of Jammu and Kashmir State; Dy. General Manager Tourism Corporation Leh etc. After retirement he was elected President of Ladakh Muslim Association, thereafter he remained at this post for several years. During his presidentship, relation between Muslims and Buddhists became normal. He supported the movement of Antonomous Hill Development Council, Leh and became the first Muslim Executive Councillor of Ladakh Autonomous Hill Development Council

Leh. Like other Muslim leaders he was inclined towards Islam and also ready to do religious works in order to upliftment Islam in Ladakh. At last on 28th June 1996 he passed away at the age of 70ys and was burried at Thiksey grave yard.

Akhon Mohd. Raza of Sheh

He was the son of Akhon Fatahullah of Sheh. His forefather came from Knour, Kargil. He received basic education from his father and Akhon Mohammad of Chuchot Yokma village later he went to Chuchot Gongma to get further education from Agha Syed Abdul Rasool. Besides Islamic education he got formal education up to Middle standard from State Govt. school. He was very intellegent and good orator. His speeches were very influencial. He often used the quotations of Allama Iqbal. During Muharram his speeches and Masias burn the heart of people. He was a bold person and never hisitate to justify the genuine cause of people.

In the beginning he worked as a Supervisor in the Public works Department. Later he resigned from the post and joined politics in 1959. He hold a good politician posts such as – President of District Congress Committee-I, President Anyumani Imamia and President Ladakh Muslim Association. He died on 15th August 1990 at the age of 69ys. and burried at Sheh grave yard.

In Conclusion Islam propogated in Ladakh initially by Islamic missionary, later through Mirza Haider and Aurangzeb, Buddhists of Ladakh embraced Islam. When King Jamyang Namgyal ('Jam-dbyans-rnam-rgyal) became the King of Ladakh, two chiefs-Ts'e-riṅ Malik of Cig-tan and another chief of Purig started quarrelling with each other. The new king immidiately went to Lower Ladakh to solve the problems. His presence provoked the intervation of Ali Mir. He was defeted and taken to Skardo prison. Later when Yabgo Sher Ghazi married his daughter with King Jamyang Namgyal. Ali Mir returned Ladakh Kingdom to King Jamyang and allowed him to rule over Ladakh. Queen rGyal khatun too came in Ladakh alongwith some Balti Muslims, who latter settled down in Phyang and Chuchot villages and, after marrying Ladakhi Buddhist girls they help to propogate Islam. Gradually Kashmiri also married Buddhist girls and helped to increase the Muslim population in Ladakh.

NOTES & REFERENCES

1. Petech, Lucians : 'The Kingdom of Ladakh C. 950-1842 A.D', Serie Orientale Roma li, 1977, P. 22

2. Sultan Zain-ul-Abidin rulled Kashmir during (1420-1470)
3. Sheh = Shey : It was old capital of Ladakh
4. Petech, Lucians; Op.cit., P. 23
5. Little Tibet : Baltistan & Great Tibet : Ladakh;
6. Cf. Petech, Luciano; Op.cit., P. 26
7. Mīrzā Haidar Dughlāt invaded Ladakh in 1532. This time Mīrzā Haidar party attacked Purig side. The Ladakh army was headed by the *jo* Bāghān.
8. Petech, Luciano; Op.cit., P. 27
9. Ibid., P. 28
10. Ibid.
11. Hor forces : Probably Turks from Yarkand or Kashgar.
12. Petech, Luciano; Op.cit., P. 30
13. Ali Mir (or Ali Khan) : He was the chief or *dmag-dpon* of Skardo
14. Petech, Luciano; Op.cit., PP.63-64
15. Ibrahim Khan was the governor of Kashmir (1678-1685)
16. sNe-mo = Ṇimo (= Nemo)
17. Petech, Luciano; Op.cit., PP. 74-80
18. Ibid., P.92
19. Ibid.
20. Ibid., P. 115
21. Ibid., PP.115-16
22. Ibid., P.117
23. Ibid., P.122
24. Ibid.
25. Ibid., P.129

BIBLIOGRAPHY

Aprem Mer : 'Nestrorian Missions' Trichur, Mar Narsai Press, 1976

Bray, John : 'The Morvian Church in Ladakh : The First forty year, 1885-1925, Detlef kantowsky (ed.)' In : 'Recent Research on Ladakh : History, Culture, Sociology, Ecology, London; Weltforum Verlag Munchan-Koln. 1981.

Das, Sarat Chandra : 'Early History of Tibet', In : Encyclopaedia of Tibet', Sharma, S.K. & Sharma, Usha (ed.); Vol. I, 1996

Francke, A.H. : 'Antiquities of Indian Tibet', S. chand & co., New Delhi.

Francke, A.H. : 'The Mysterious Land', Ess-Ess, Pub., New Delhi, 1980.

Gazetteer of Kashmir and Ladak(h) : Vivek Pub. House, Delhi, 1974.

Gargan, Yoseb : 'Ladags Rgyalrabs Chimed Ster' (History of Ladakh), New Delhi, Sterling Pub., 1976.

Jina, Prem Singh : 'Ladakh Aur Paryatan' (Tourism in Ladakh), In : Ist National Conference, C.I.B.S., Leh - Ladakh, 1981.

Jina, Prem Singh : 'Ladakh ki Sanskriti per Seemeant Sanskriti ka Prabhav', New letter, New Delhi, Sept-Oct. 1982.

Jina, Prem Singh : 'Bhagwan Buddha Kaha', Dinman, Times of India, Pub., New Delhi, 28th Nov. 4th Dec. 1982.

Jina, Prem Singh : 'Santi Stupa Ladakh Ke', Yojana, Jammu; March, 1983.

Jina, Prem Singh : 'Boudh Bhiksus of Ladakh', In : Proceed of All India Conference; Delhi University, Delhi, 1983.

Jina, Prem Singh : 'Seet kal me Leh Ghati', Sheeraja-65, Jammu, March - 1983

Jina, Prem Singh : The Foreign Tourist Traffic in Ladakh; Himalayan Research and Development (Problem Oriented Studies), Vol.3(i) Nainital, June, 1984.

Jina Prem Singh : Buddhism in Ladakh and World Peace; In 10th International Buddhist Conference on Buddhism and World Peace, Japanese Temple, Bodh Gaya, Vol-X; 1984

Jina, Prem Singh : 'Astangik Marg aur Moksa', Prakasitman, Delhi, March 1984

Jina, Prem Singh : 'Foreign tourists and their impact on Ladakh', In IIIrd National Conference Proceed., Ladakh Prabh (3), 1985

Jina, Prem Singh : 'A Brief Introduction of Ladakh Gonpas', In : Ladakh : Life & Culture'; K.N. Pandit (ed.), Kashmir University, Srinagar; 1986, PP. 39-50

Jina, Prem Singh : 'Economic & Cultural Relations between Ladakh and Lahul & Spiti', In : Ist All India Conference, at Baudh Darshan Mahavidayalaya, Keylong, (H.P.)

Jina, Prem Singh : 'A Survey of Buddhist Community in Ladakh Himalaya' In : 12th International Buddhist Conference on Buddhism and Social Harmony, Japanese Temple, Bodh Gaya, India, Vol. XII, 1986

Jina, Prem Singh : Pasturelands of Zangskar and its effects on Ecology : In Ist National Conference, Leh-Ladakh, 1986

Jina, Prem Singh & Mir, A.A. : Pasturelands of Leh and its effects on Ecology in Ist National Conference Organised by Indian Army, Trishul Nature Conservation, Leh-Ladakh, 1986.

Jina, Prem Singh : Monasteries in the Economy of Leh - Ladakh, In : All India Conference on Buddhist Monasteries of Himalayan Region : Various Aspect; 9-13th August, CIBS, Leh, 1988

Jina, Prem Singh : Bodh Dham Leh-Ladakh, Hindu Chetana, Vol.-7, New Delhi, June, 1988, PP.21-33

Jina, Prem Singh : 'Ladakhi Rajao ka Bodh Dharm me Yogdan', Hindu

Chetana, Vol. 10, Sept. 1988, PP. 19-20

Jina, Prem Singh : 'Eco-Environmental Study of tourist industry in Ladakh Himalaya; In : All India Conference, Kashmir University, Srinagar, Deptt. of Centre for Central Asian Studies, 1989.

Jina, Prem Singh : 'Pashimna Economy in Ladakh', Yojana, Delhi, Dec. 1990, PP. 13-16

Jina, Prem Singh : 'Pasture Ecology of Leh-Ladakh', In : Wissenschalts Gegschichte and Gegenwarlige Forschungen in Nordwest Indian staatliches Muslim fur Volkerkunde, Dresden Forschungsstelle, Germany, 1990

Jina, Prem Singh : Ladakh me Bodh Kala ka Udbhav aur Wikash; Sheeraja Feb.-March., Vol., 1991, PP. 12-14

Jina, Prem Singh : 'History & Growth of Education; Himalaya Today, Nov. 1991, PP.16-18

Jina, Prem Singh : 'Ladakhi Shirobhusa - Perakh', Seeraja, Feb.–March, Vol. 6, 1992, PP. 20-23

Jina, Prem Singh : 'Ladakh Ki Mahila Prashashak Putith Wangmo', Hamara Sahitya, Jammu, 1992, PP. 104-106.

Jina, Prem Singh : 'Impact of Tourism on Ladakhi Society and Culture', In : All India Conference, J.N.U., New Delhi, 1993

Jina, Prem Singh : 'Poultry Industry in Ladakh Himalayan', Himalaya Today, Sept., 92-Feb. 1993 Vol. IX, No. 2 & 3, 1993, P. 7.

Jina, Prem Singh : Dasvi Satabdi Purva Lahul me Bodh Dharm evam Sanskriti, Janjati Mela Smarika; 1993, PP. 60-62

Jina, Prem Singh : 'Tourism in Ladakh Himalaya', Indus Publishing Company, New Delhi, 1994

Jina, Prem Singh : 'Tourist Industry in Ladakh', Himalaya Today, Jan-March, Vol. IV, No.2, New Delhi, 1994, P. 20

Jina, Prem Singh & Konchok Namgyal : 'Spiti Ka Sanskratik Itihas; Janjati Utsava, 1994, PP. 70-72

Jina, Prem Singh : Buddhism in Ladakh and its Approach to the Material World; In : Buddhism Approach to Material World; Proceed of the 18th International Buddhist Conference, Vol. XVIII; Bodh Gya, 1993-

94, PP. 51-60

Jina, Prem Singh : Bhiksuni Sangha Avam Ladakh me Usaki Stithi', Proceed of the National Conference 1994, PP. 50-52.

Jina, Prem Singh : Kesar ka Mahakaviya, Sheeraja, Vol. II, June-July, Jammu, 1994

Jina, Prem Singh : High Pasturelands of Ladakh Himalaya, Indus Pub. Co., New Delhi, 1995

Jina, Prem Singh & Konechok Namgyal : 'Phyang Monastery of Ladakh', Indus Pub. Co., New Delhi, 1995

Jina, Prem Singh : 'Famous Western Explorers to Ladakhi', Indus Pub. Co., New Delhi, 1995

Jina, Prem Singh : 'Buddhism in Ladakh', Yug Udbodhan, Vol. I, No. 9, New Delhi, 1995, PP. 14-16.

Jina, Prem Singh : 'Ladakh : The Land and the people', Indus Pub. Co., New Delhi, 1996

Jina, Prem Singh : 'Hemis' The Biggest Buddhist Monastery of Ladakh', Yug Udbodhan, Vol. 2, No. 4, New Delhi, 1996., P. 15

Jina, Prem Singh : 'Ladakhi Gonpao me Bhiksuo ki Pravesh Vidhi', Yug Udbodhan; Vol. 2, No. 6., New Delhi; 1996, P. 9.

Jina, Prem Singh : 'Tabo Monastery– A Unique Menument in Spiti Valley; Yug Udbodhan, Vol.2, No. 11, New Delhi, Nov. 1996, P. 13.

Jina, Prem Singh (ed.) : 'Recent Researchers on the Himalaya', Indus Pub. Co., New Delhi, 1997

Jina, Prem Singh : 'Tibetan Manuscripts and Inscriptions on Ladakh Himalaya', Sri Guru Pub., New Delhi, 1998

Jina, Prem Singh : 'Some Monasteries of Drigung pa Order in Central Ladakh', Sri Guru Pub., New Delhi, 1999

Jina, Prem Singh : 'Changing Face of Ladakh Himalaya', Om Pub., New Delhi, 1999

Jina, Prem Singh & Konchok Namgyal : 'Lamayuru Monastery of Ladakh Himalaya', Om Pub., New Delhi, 1999.

Jina, Prem Singh : 'Ladakh Mera Anubhav' (My Experience in Ladakh), Anjuri, 1999

Jina, Prem Singh : 'Ladakhi Kala Avam Sanskriti' (In Press)

Jina, Prem Singh : 'History of Education and growth in Ladakh', Paper presented in the International Conference, IALS, Leh-Ladakh, 1999.

Khan, Hasmatullah : 'Tarike Jammu', 1939

Khosla, Sarla : 'History of Buddhism in Kashmir', Sagar Pub., New Delhi, 1972 .

Kundan, T.Z. : 'A Christian from Ladakh Bobility : Elijah Thsetan Phuntog', In : 'Christianity in Jammu & Kashmir', Kashmir, Vishinath Press, PP. 80-81

Menon, Appan : 'Lessons from Ladakh', Frontline, July 28- August 4, 1989.

Nawang Tsering : 'Buddhism in Ladakh', Sterling Pub., New Delhi, 1979

Petech, Luciano : 'The Kingdom of Ladakh C 950-1842 A.D.', Serie Oriental Roma li, 1977

Peter, Celetine : "A report of Visit to Leh, 24-29 August", 1992

Peter, Celetine : "Mission Ladakh", 1994 Motilal Banarasidas Pub., Delhi; 1987

Rizvi, Janet : 'Ladakh : Crossroads of High Asia', Oxford University Press, Delhi.

Sharma, S.K. & Sharma, Usha (ed.) : 'Encyclopaedia of Tibet Vol. I, 1996.

Sykes, Perry : 'A History of Exploration', London, 1934

Thirunilath, Dominic : 'A Cursory Glance of the Early History of Christianity', In : Christianity of Jammu & Kashmir, Kashmir, Vishinath Press.

Vadakel, Sebastian : 'A Pilgrimage to Tangtse on the Chinese Boarder', Santhome Mission, Vol. III, No. 4., 1996

Vohra, Rohit : 'Dating of a Maitreya Relief of the Mid-8th Century : from Sumda Chen'; South Asian Studies, 1993.

Vries, Sjoered-Jande: 'Notes on the History and Iconography of Bakula'; In : Recent Research on Ladakh', London 1983.

Upasak, C.S. : 'Early Buddhism in Ladakh', In : 'Ladakh Prabha', Kendriya Buddha Vidya Sansthan, Leh-Ladakh, 1986

Wessels, C : 'Early Jesuit Travellers in Central Asia', Book Faith India, Delhi, 1998.

INDEX